Sermons for 18 Special Occasions

Publishing House
St. Louis

3558 South Jefferson Avenue, St. Louis, MO 63118

Manufactured in the United States of America

Library of Congress Cataloging in Publication Data

Main entry under title:
Sermons for 18 special occasions.

Sermons by pastors of the Lutheran Church—Missouri Synod.
1. Occasional sermons. 2. Sermons, American. 3. Lutheran Church—Sermons. I. Lutheran Church—Missouri Synod. II. Title: Sermons for eighteen special occasions.
BV4254.2.S425 1983 252'.6 82-8272
ISBN 0-570-03870-7 (pbk.)

---

1 2 3 4 5 6 7 8 9 10 IB 92 91 90 89 88 87 86 85 84 83

PREFACE

A busy preacher can never have enough preaching aids—especially when emergencies arise, time is limited, and inspiration does not come easily. For those special times that are not covered in annual collections of sermons based on the church year or revolving around a single theme, this gathering of 20 sermons is being offered for 18 special occasions, with two sermons each for weddings and funerals.

An additional feature of this volume is the listing of parallel texts and/or Scripture readings and suggested hymns to fit each sermon.

May these sermons provide a fitting Gospel word to the special occasions that occur in the lives of God's people.

The Publisher

CONTENTS

50TH CHURCH ANNIVERSARY

Our Joy Is in Remembering and Sharing

1 CHRON. 16:8-12

This is a great day for you, the members and former members of Bethany Lutheran Church. You have made it known that you are celebrating the 50th anniversary of the founding of your congregation. That makes your church older than the average member. Many of you know the early history of Bethany only from the stories told by a few remaining charter members.

But what a joy it is to hear the accounts of those who so vividly remember the courage and the faith it took to start a new congregation. What they remember even more is the joy they shared. Isn't that true of all anniversaries?

Our Joy Is in Remembering and Sharing

Truly, *anniversaries are for those who want to remember.* That is brought out most clearly in the text that was read. This beautiful hymn of praise which I chose as the Scriptural basis of my address was written by a king. King David, who wrote it, wanted his whole kingdom to rejoice in the blessings of the Lord. His hymn of praise was written to help his people to remember the blessings. May it help you today to remember and thus to rejoice in the blessings of the Lord enjoyed in Bethany in these past 50 years.

Much of the joy in an anniversary celebration comes through careful preparation for the event. King David was a master of that. He wanted to bring the ark of the covenant to Jerusalem that it might be a constant reminder of God's love and mercy for His people. So he caused a beautiful tabernacle to be erected to house the ark. He engaged the services of 865 priests and Levites to officiate at the celebration. Many of them offered sacrifices. Others sang in a large choir or accompanied the choir with harps and lyres, trumpets and cymbals. To add to the festivities, King David gave orders that every person who attended was to be given a portion of meat from the animals sacrificed, a loaf of bread, a flagon of wine. Some of the translations say it was a raisin cake, not a flagon of wine. I felt I should leave that an open question.

And who were the guests at this great celebration? David invited all the brethren left in all the land of Israel to come. And they came. The holy writer says: "All Israel brought up the ark of the covenant of the Lord with shouting, to the sound of the horn, trumpets, and cymbals, and made loud music on harps and lyres" (1 Chron. 15:28).

The 50th anniversary of the founding of Bethany Lutheran Church is not as grand an event as was the celebration arranged by King David, but I am sure your arrangement committee did all they could to add to the festivities of this day. For this service of praise is only a part of your celebration. Much of the sharing of remembrances has already taken place and will continue through the days to come.

But nothing that you do to celebrate your 50th anniversary is more important than the service itself. May David's hymn of praise help you to see that.

The holy writer calls on us first of all to focus on the reason for praising the Lord. For David the ark itself was reason enough. It was called the ark of the covenant. It was constantly to remind Israel of the covenant God had made to send Christ into the world to save not only the people of Israel but all who would follow them in faith. The cover of the ark was called the mercy seat. Israel was to remember God as a merciful Savior, forgiving their sins, keeping them in the faith, assuring them of a place in heaven. The mercy seat covered the tables of stone on which the Ten Commandments were written, to remind Israel that the transgressions against God's holy law would all be forgiven if they trusted in God's mercy, which He could show them because He would send Christ to die for their sins.

Surely every one of you attending this service of praise remembers only too well how often you have sinned against the Lord. Yet His mercy has been proclaimed to you every time you come to church. The altar that was set up in your first place of worship 50 years ago was a simple table, covered with tapestry. Yet it was just as faithful a reminder of the sacrifice Christ brought for our sins as is the beautiful altar in your church today. The font at which many of you were baptized held the water which through God's holy Word washed away your sins and made you children of God. On this 50th anniversary of the founding of your church, be sure to remember that you are a baptized child of God and thus an heir of salvation. Remember also that over the past 50 years thousands of others were brought to the Lord in Holy Baptism, many of them joining you today to sing praise to the Lord for His mercy.

You surely will also remember to praise the Lord for the thousands of sermons preached to your congregation since it was founded. How can I possibly do justice to the importance of those sermons, in which God spoke to you through your pastors? Every teaching recorded in the Word had a message especially for you. You were reminded again and again that God, who had created the world, the sun, the moon, and stars, also made you, giving you a body and soul, eyes, ears, and all your members, your reason and all your senses, and still preserving them. Thank God with me right now for reminding you that if you can see the flowers on the altar it is because God gave you the gift of sight. If you can hear the anthems sung to His praise in this service of worship, it is because God gave you the gift of hearing. If your heart is thrilling at the thought that you had a part in the growth of Bethany, it is because God filled your heart with faith and love and gave you a mind to dwell on His great work of creation.

And what shall I say of the sermons that dealt with your salvation, your eternal election, your justification? Would you now be able to say that Jesus is your Lord, who redeemed you with His holy precious blood, if He had not reminded you of His love? Think also of the sermons that helped you to understand the life that is pleasing to God and the help He constantly gives you to live your life to His glory.

Would you be able to control your anger, your fleshly appetites, your evil desires, if God had not spoken to you through the years, pointing out your sins and assuring you of the power to resist them?

Think of the sermons that dwelt on the blessings in the marriages of Christian couples, the love husband and wife can show each other, because God has filled them with His love; the sermons that fostered Christian education of your children; the sermons preached at the funerals of loved ones, with the assurance they gave you of the resurrection of your body and the life you will live with God.

Let your 50th anniversary serve to remind you of how blessed you have been to be a member of a Christian congregation that saw to the proper use of the sacraments and the proper preaching of the Word, that you might live a happy life, honored to be one of God's saints on earth. What reason you have in this service of praise to join your fellow Christians in thanking God for His mercy, His love, and His help!

But King David will tell you that your celebration is not complete if it is just a service of thanksgiving to your gracious Lord.

Remembrances should be shared—and not only with your fellow Christians. David says: "Make known His deeds among the peoples!" He is referring to other nations.

That should help you to understand God's ways in the Old Testament. When He chose the people of Israel as the nation from whom Christ would be born, He did not turn His back on all other nations. He was not willing that other nations should perish. He wanted Israel to help other nations to know the true God and to believe in Him. David makes that very clear in his hymn of praise when he says that Israel should make God's deeds known to the other nations. That means all other nations. Egypt, for instance, had 400 years to learn about the true God because the Israelites lived in their land. As Israel traveled from Egypt to Palestine, all the nations on the way had a chance to learn about the true God. In the years that David was king,

God gave him control over other nations. They could then have learned to know about David's God and Savior, who is also our God and Savior.

Remember, as you celebrate this day, that Jesus died for all people. And He wants all people to hear about Him. That is why Bethany from the very beginning of its existence contributed to the mission work of the Synod. That handful of charter members could have said: We need all of our offerings for ourselves. But they knew better. They saw their little group as part of a large church, with opportunity to spread the Word of God in many, many parts of the world.

Try to see that after 50 years you have reached the point where you should be able to increase your offerings for your Synod's work from year to year, so that you can thus reach out to others as others through their contributions have reached out to you.

Our knowledge of other nations, our knowledge of the false gods they worship, should help us to realize how great the task still is. Under the blessing of God, Bethany has become a large congregation, able to do great things for the work of the Lord. In this anniversary service, as you praise God for His blessings, ask Him to give you a heart of love for others that they may share in the blessings you enjoy.

What joy you will find in such work! What proof you will be giving to others that the blessings you now enjoy are important to you!

One final thought. David says in his hymn of praise: "Seek His presence continually." Don't ever become so sure of yourselves that you forget how dependent you are on God. That I say to you as a congregation on your 50th anniversary and to every one of you who hold membership in Bethany. Remember the words of your Savior: "Apart from Me you can do nothing."

David knew that so well by his bitter experiences in life. When he failed to follow the Lord, whom he called his Shepherd, he became involved in sins that stagger our imagination. He became guilty of adultery, murder, deceit, and almost lost his kingdom.

But God in His mercy brought David back into the fold and blessed him abundantly, making him the greatest king that Israel ever had. He not only ruled well. He also provided the world with psalms and hymns that are a comfort and assurance for us as they are for all who today can say with us: "The Lord is my Shepherd. . . . I shall dwell in the house of the Lord forever."

Bethany is your house now. Here Christ is speaking to you, nourishing you, strengthening you, forgiving you, and living in you. Oh, then glory in His name. Seek His presence continually. Remember His wonderful works. Make them known throughout the world, that others may rejoice with you, as you add year to year in your joyful service to the Lord. May He bless you abundantly on this day of celebration and in the days to come, in Jesus Christ your Lord.

Mark J. Steege

Related Scripture Readings

1 Kings 8:26-30
Ps. 66:1-4
Ps. 89:1-7, 15-18
Ps. 100
Is. 2:2-5
1 Peter 2:4-10
Jude 20-25

Suggested Hymns

"Songs of Praise the Angels Sang"
"Hark! The Church Proclaims Her Honor"
"I Love Thy Kingdom, Lord"
"Christ, Thou Art the Sure Foundation"
"We Praise Thee, O God, Our Redeemer, Creator"
"Let Children Hear the Mighty Deeds"
"Great Is the Lord, Our God"
"God the Father, Son, and Spirit"
"Praise to God, Immortal Praise"
"Only-Begotten, Word of God Eternal"
"Thy Strong Word Did Cleave the Darkness"
"O Thou, Who Hast of Thy Pure Grace"
"O Fearful Place, Where He Who Knows Our Heart"

BACCALAUREATE/GRADUATION

God's Advice to Youth

ECCL. 12:1

The Holy Scriptures are filled with many exhortations and words of counsel that are directed in a general way to all people. Some sections of the Bible, however, have words of advice aimed at specific groups, such as the elderly, or men, or women. There are some admonitions of Scripture addressed specifically to parents. Our text is distinctive in that it is specifically addressed not to adults, not to little children, but to youth.

What Is God's Advice?

This is a very appropriate text for this occasion as we are gathered to honor the youth of this graduating class who have successfully completed this segment of their schooling and have earned their diplomas. What does God's Word have to say today to you who stand at this very important crossroad in your lifetime? What does God have to say to you who are so young and so full of the vigor and strength of youth; to you who are so filled with energy, enthusiasm, and zest for living? To you who think young because you are young, God says these words: "Remember now thy Creator in the days of thy youth" (KJV).

God is saying, "Think about Me now while you are young." Become concerned about God and His will. Be concerned about religion now. Don't put it off until you are old and gray, but be concerned about it now while it can still do you the greatest amount of good during your lifetime; while you can still reap the biggest benefits and inherit the greatest number of years of blessings as a disciple of our Lord.

One Youth's Plan

Some years ago while traveling I met a high school student and began talking to him about his plans for the future and about the place of God and the church in his life. He appeared to be a bright lad who expressed himself well and was very much involved in the activities of his high school. In fact, he was so busy he said that he just didn't have time for religion in his life. He said he was not really against God and the church but what with athletics, parties, a job, school work, taking care of his car, etc., there was just no time left for the church and religious activities. He said he was not opposed to God but he just wanted to postpone involvement for awhile until he got a little older. His life's plan went something like this:

First of all, he said, he wanted to go to college and get a good education and prepare for a career. Next he planned to get his military obligation out of the way since those were the days of the draft. Then he hoped to get a good job, settle down, and get married. "Then," he said, "I plan to join a church and get involved with religion again."

What unmitigated folly this young man spoke! What he was actually planning to do was to make three of the most important decisions of his life without the help and guidance of God and His holy Word. He was going to choose a college and a career, go through the hazards of military service probably far away from home, and then he was going to select his life's mate, a wife, and after all these important decisions were made, then he was going to turn to God and the church.

The young man reminded me very much of a person who was saying, "I am going to build a large house. First I am going to select a site. Then I will gather many materials and hire laborers and begin building. And when it is rather well begun, then I will have time to begin consulting with an architect or a planning engineer." What he failed to understand is that God is the best architect for young lives. God is the master builder of lives and careers. The Bible says: "Except the Lord build the house, they labor in vain that build it" (Ps. 127:1 KJV). It is so important to begin your planning for the future with God now. It is so important to begin building your life, your career, your vocation, your marriage, and your home with God and His counsel. One of the great hymns in our hymn book says: "With the Lord begin thy task, Jesus will direct it; For His aid and counsel ask, Jesus will perfect it." The Bible says: "The fear of the Lord is the beginning of wisdom." That's where real wisdom begins, with God. God is the Source of all true wisdom. So all those who want to make a good beginning as they plan for their future will begin their planning with God.

Many of you will be continuing your studies in another school or college. Some of you may be planning to go to work or into special job training. Whatever decisions or choices face you, God is saying to all of you, "Now is the time, while you are young, to lay the important foundation stones for a spiritual life. Now is the time to form the lifelong habits of daily Bible reading and prayer. Now is the time to take a stand for God and for His Son, our Savior Jesus Christ. Now is the time to chart the course of your life. Now is the time to make a commitment of faith and a confession with the boldness and courage of a young Joshua of the Old Testament who, as he was about to take over the reigns of leadership, was not unduly influenced by the indecision of others around him but said boldly: 'As for me and my house, we will serve the Lord.' "

"Remember"

Our text is a short one, but every word of it is important. Let us carefully examine each of the key words. The first word is "Remember." God is not saying to youth, "Please remember" or "Remember, if you have time." He is giving you a divine command. He is issuing you an order! The grammatical construction used here is an imperative. It is the same form we would use to say, "Close that window!" Or, "Open that door!" God expects us to carry out His will when He speaks to us.

"Remember" also means to recall to mind, to think about, to ponder, to meditate. "Remember" is also a way of saying, "Don't forget." God says, "Don't forget about Me." Don't forget about me in the hustle and bustle of the busy and active days of youth. This admonition is particularly appropriate for you young people who are well acquainted with God and who have been baptized in a Christian church and confirmed at its altars. You who have pledged your faithfulness to Him as His disciples, as His members and His soldiers; you who know His Son, Jesus Christ, as your personal Savior; you who are aware that Christ suffered and died for your sins on the cross and has earned for you eternal life—You are His. God is saying in effect in our text, "Remember that and don't ever forget it!" He is saying, "Remember how much I love you individually. Remember I will never leave you or forsake you and I will never forget you. 'Behold, I have graven thee upon the palms of my hand.' 'Can a woman forget her sucking child, that she should not have compassion on the son of her womb? Yea, they may forget, yet will I not forget thee' " (Is. 49:15-16 KJV). This great remembering love of God which He has for us in Christ Jesus also constrains us to remember Him.

"Now"

And when does God want you to remember Him and think about Him? A few years from now? Next month? Someday when you have time? No. God says it in one unmistakably clear word, *"Now!"* God knows the temperament of youth. He knows that youth like action and involvement right now and that they are often impatient with the slower-moving pace of the adult world. The youth of today have been characterized in modern literature as the "now generation." These words from God challenge the action-oriented "now generation" to act right now—not when you are old, but now during the days of your youthfulness: "Remember now thy Creator in the days of thy youth." Don't try to live your life as if God doesn't exist. Don't postpone confrontation with God. Don't try to avoid the spiritual dimension of your life.

Remember Him who not only created you but who also died for you on Calvary's cross. Remember the good news that He loved you from eternity and has called you to faith by and through the power of the Gospel of His Son Jesus Christ. Most of all remember His gracious promise that He who has begun this good work of creating faith in you will go on performing it until the day of Christ's return.

"Thy Creator"

And what does God want you to remember about Him? He wants you to remember that He is your creator. God is in effect saying, "Hey, remember who I am. I made the universe and all that is in it. I created all things. I created you. I have given you your body and soul and all your talents and skills. I have created all living things, and I preserve and protect them. Without Me you can do nothing. So don't forget about Me."

God knows youth are busy, but He also knows that in your very busyness you need Him. In the excitement and vigor of youth, in the venture of growing up and maturing, in the thrill of falling in love, in the joys of courtship, engagement, and marriage, in the activity of high school and college and preparing for a career, in all of this God says, "I want you to 'remember now thy Creator.' "

God would have you consider that He is not only the Creator of physical life; He is also the Source and Creator of spiritual life. He gives us as a free gift the faith we need to believe His promises. He gives us forgiveness of sins, life and salvation, and He strengthens us spiritually to meet the temptations of life. That is why we pray, "Create in me a clean heart, O God, and renew a right spirit within me" (Ps. 51:10 KJV).

There used to be a cliche expression that said, "The youth of today are the church of tomorrow." When I was your age I used to hear that statement often from my elders. Thank God that today we are saying more accurately, "The youth of today are also the church of today." You are just as much a part of the church as any adult member. Your membership in the church is just as important as the membership of your parents. This is so because we are all members of the body of Christ and we are all one in Christ Jesus. As members of His body there is no distinction between master or slave, man or woman, Jew or Gentile, white or black, young or old. You are an important part of the church right now. Remember it.

Youth are the greatest natural resource that our nation possesses. This is true simply because people are the greatest resource a nation possesses and youth are people who probably have most of their life still ahead of them. Youth are just as important as adults. They are not less important even though sometimes they have been treated that way. That is wrong. In recent years some people have treated youth as though they were more important than adults. That too is wrong. We are on the right track when we understand and heed the Scriptural statement: "You are all one in Christ Jesus" (Gal. 3:28). There is no difference or importance or status before God. In the church we are all absolute equals—equally sinful and equally forgiven by the same undeserved grace and mercy of God in Christ Jesus. That message of undeserved grace and mercy which guarantees the forgiveness of all of our sin in Christ Jesus is the good news that God wants us to remember not only for our own sake but also to share freely with the entire world.

"In the Days of Thy Youth"

Thousands of young graduates like you all over our country are swiftly growing up and maturing and will soon be young adults. The years of transition from childhood and adolescence to full maturity are one of the more difficult times of life. In addition to all the usual problems of physical change and social adjustment, you will face all the temptations that young people of every generation have always faced. You will face the usual temptations of dishonesty, cheating, slovenliness, or laziness. You will face the same youthful temptations of sexual immorality that young people have always faced.

Your generation, however, will encounter some differences in the world around you. You are living in a world that is in confusion. Many old traditional values and standards have crumbled during the past two decades. You will be able to read many articles even in popular magazines which will suggest to you that the old codes of morality are outdated and irrelevant in these modern times. Today there are voices saying that there is a "new morality." You will hear some voices in the world saying that the sexual behavior which has always been proper and ethical only within the bounds of God's holy institution of marriage may now be practiced by the unmarried. You will hear other voices in the world saying that all the old standards of conduct preached and taught by the Christian church can be disregarded.

Some voices are even still echoing the outmoded cliché expression and saying, "God is dead."

But the followers of Jesus Christ, whether young or old, do not follow the voices of this world, especially when those voices speak things contrary to what God says in His Word. Christian people remember God and remember what He says. I know that you as Christian youth regard the Ten Commandments as I do, not as the obsolete will of a dead God, but as the holy, absolute will of the living God. Christians are concerned, of course, not only about God's Ten Commandments but also about all that God has to tell them and teach them in His Word.

To remember God is also to remember His Word. In a setting such as this I cannot help but recall God's advice to young Timothy, written by the apostle Paul. Paul told Timothy in effect these same things I have been saying to you. He wrote that Timothy should continue in what he had learned about God, and should remember His Word, which could lead him to eternal life through faith in Christ Jesus. Remember God now in the days of your youth. That is more than just a good idea, more than just a nice-sounding motto. It is a word of advice and direction from God Himself. It is a word of counsel on which you can build your future life with confidence.

But what is it that will enable you to remember your Creator and to fight the good fight and stand against all the attacks and temptations of the devil, the world, and your flesh? It is not your own strength or cunning or the energy of youth. No indeed. Rather it is the armor and power that God Himself supplies for you through His Word. It is the power of the Gospel of Jesus Christ which equips you with "the breastplate of righteousness . . . the helmet of salvation . . . the sword of the spirit . . . the shield of faith" (Eph. 6:14-17). May the Holy Spirit of God continue to create in you a clean heart and renew your spirit daily so that you may be enabled to remember Him and the good news of His free salvation for you through His Son, our Lord Jesus Christ. Amen.

Michael J. Stelmachowicz

Related Scripture Readings

Prov. 2:1-15
Prov. 3:11-18
Prov. 4:1-13
1 Tim. 4:11—5:2
Titus 2
1 John 2:12-17

Suggested Hymns

"Creator Spirit, by Whose Aid"
"Glorious Things of Thee Are Spoken"
"Shepherd of Tender Youth"

CHRISTIAN EDUCATION

House of Life

DEUT. 11:18-21; EPH. 3:14-19

Hetty Green was one of the richest women in the history of the United States. In 1900, when the average income in this country was $490 a year, her income was seven million dollars. When she died in 1916, she left an estate of 200 million dollars. Yes, Hetty Green was well known for her incredible wealth—and for her incredible greed and stinginess. In Boston, when her young son developed an infection in his leg, she went to a public clinic to have it treated. When they discovered who she was, they asked her to pay for it. She refused. She took him to one public clinic after the next, and each time the scene was repeated. She postponed treating the leg so long, trying to avoid paying for it, that the infection reached the point that there was no other alternative—her son's leg had to be amputated.

Such a thing seems unbelievable, incredible to us. How could anyone do such a thing? I wonder what impression she left on her son. I wonder what she built her life on.

Jesus said: "Everyone who hears these words of Mine and does not do them will be like a foolish man who built his house upon the sand; and the rain fell, and the floods came, and the winds blew and beat against that house, and it fell; and great was the fall of it" (Matt. 7:26-27).

There are only two ways to build a life or a house, on rock or on sand. The house built on the rock stands. It stands through the winds, through rains, it is a house of joy, a house of life! In contrast there is a house built on the sand. It is a house that is battered and broken in the end. It is full of sorrow and sadness and emptiness. It brings pain and loneliness. In the end, it is not a house of life but a house of death! None of us wants to build such a house of death. None of us wants to wait until we hear the sound of snapping timber and cracking walls to wish we had done it differently. How can we prevent such building? How do we build on the rock?

Our focus today is on Christian education. The title for this word, "House of Life," is one of the names given by the ancient people of Egypt to the schools attached to their temples. To the Hebrews also, education meant life, but only that learning which was connected to God could indeed bring life and build a house of life for the students. In contrast, the Greeks and Romans considered education to be a humanistic enterprise. Man's mind nurtured and developed, in itself, was able to discover truth and the meaning of life. But the Hebrews believed that all truth comes from God. He is the Creator, Judge, and Redeemer of man. That is where all education for life must begin and end, as the writer of Proverbs had spoken it: "The fear of the Lord is the beginning of wisdom."

How do you build a House of Life? Where do we begin? I'd like to begin with one of those parables that's been passed on from pastor to pastor.

> The telephone rang. Mrs. Waverly hurriedly picked it up. "Hello . . . Yes . . . Oh, you're Johnny's teacher," she said. "I've been meaning to call you!" She listened for a moment, and then said, "No, Johnny isn't planning to be in school this year. You see, he has so much work to do at the church—Sunday School, confirmation class, church services, youth activities, choir, and such to take up so much of his time! Then there are daily devotions at home and other interests, so there isn't any time left for school. . . .
>
> "Well, yes, I know that school is important and I know that you are doing a fine job with the children in this community—and I've been intending to write a letter of appreciation to the school about it. I surely would hate to live in a place where there was no school.
>
> "To tell you the truth, though, Mr. Earnest, Johnny didn't like school too well last year, and it interfered with his choir practice at the church. Besides, all those examinations, having to bring home a report card showing his progress—it was very embarrassing to him. He also suffered some psychological effects, for so many girls were attending school, and he thought it was sissy to go. So he decided that he just wouldn't attend school this year.
>
> "Am I going to make him go? Of course not! No, I don't think his educational growth will be harmed. Yes, if he were to decide to return to school, it would be all right with me. I just want to make sure that it's his decision. I don't want to force him into anything he doesn't want to do."

I suppose what makes the parable humorous to us is that we can't really imagine such a thing happening. For all our roots in God's tradition we often act as though God's things were not the most important things to teach our children. No, in practice, in reality, we are often closer to the old Greeks and Romans. The education that best serves our children is secular, not sacred education. That's what will pay the bills, build their homes, and prepare them for life, we say. In a backhanded way the parable also reminds us of another misconception we have. Christian education is for the children. It's good for them; who would deny that? But for me, well I'm beyond all that. Yes, these are the ways we think. They are our ways, but they are not God's ways. Listen to how the writer of Deuteronomy put it: "You shall therefore lay up these words of mine in your heart and in your soul; and you shall bind them as a sign upon your hand, and they shall be as frontlets between your eyes."

Do you want to know where you should start, the place to begin? Begin with yourself, the point at which God, too, has begun. Begin by laying up His words and ways until they burn in your heart and live in your soul. Bind them to your hands until every movement, every action is His action, a work of praise to Him. Set His words and ways between your eyes until you reach the point where you see every event, every person, everything that crosses your path as God sees it. Let His Word mold and shape you, guide and lead you. Let it be in every syllable, every breath, every heartbeat, every blink of your eye. Lay up these words of His, do them, live them—and He Himself will be your Life, your Way, and your only Reality.

Begin with yourself, where God has begun. That's what the apostle Paul did too. Paul's prayer to the congregation at Ephesus is not only plural, it is personal and singular too. It is for each of us. Listen: "May God grant you to be strengthened with might through His Spirit in the inner man, and that Christ may dwell in your hearts through faith; that you, being rooted and grounded in love, may have the power to comprehend with all the saints what is the breadth and length and height and depth, and to know the love of Christ which surpasses knowledge, that you may be filled with all the fulness of God."

Did you catch it? Did you hear the educational overtones? When Christ dwells in your heart through faith, when He lives there, rules there, remains there, when you are rooted and grounded, held in place and secured in His love, then you will have power to comprehend with all the saints what is the breadth and length and height and depth. Jesus Christ is the very Wisdom of God, the Logos, the Divine Word who was before all things, made all things, and holds together all things. When you grow in Christ and are anchored and centered in Him, you will be able to comprehend the mystery of God that is behind creation and beyond all breadth and length, height and depth. You will know something more than any man or any earthbound institution can teach you. You will know the love of Christ, which surpasses knowledge.

You see, Paul is talking about the doctoral program in discipleship and the mysteries of God that begins at baptism. He is talking about a doctoral program in building a House of Life. Throughout His letters he draws the blueprints:

—Let your roots grow deep, strong, and secure
—"Let your manner of life be worthy of the Gospel of Christ."
—"Try to learn what is pleasing to the Lord."
—"Press on toward the goal for the prize of the upward call of God in Christ Jesus."
—Learn to "walk in love, as Christ loved us and gave Himself up for us."
—Grow up "to the measure of the stature of the fulness of Christ."
—Learn the secret of facing plenty and hunger, abundance and want;
—Learn to be content in whatever state you are.
—Learn that you can do all things in Him who strengthens you.
—Yes, press on, that you may be filled with all the fulness of God!

"You shall therefore lay up these words of mine in your heart and in your soul; and you shall bind them as a sign upon your hand, and they shall be as frontlets between your eyes. *And you shall teach them to your children. . . .*" The circle of education now moves beyond me to the children around me. It had to begin with me. Unless I make this laying up of the words of God my own, for my own life and necessity, how are the children to believe that these words are the words of life for them too? There is no way that we can speak of these words of God when we are sitting in our house, when we are walking by the way, or when we lie down and when we rise unless they are part of us.

We learn by example; that is why, again and again, Paul would say: "Join in imitating me"; do what I do. Children, too, learn by example. A little quote from "Friendly Thoughts" wisely says: "You teach little by what you say, but more by what you are." Or as some unknown but obviously perceptive parishioner put it: "I'd rather see a sermon then hear one."

If forgiveness is important, share it. If love is important, show it. If you want to teach your children that church is important, be there. If you want them to know Christ's Meal as God's means of grace, then kneel here. And if you feel that these words of God are important for your children, then speak them, study them, digest them. Yes, if Christ is the Way, the Truth, the Life, then follow Him and teach Him to your children.

What do we teach that is of life-and-death importance for the children? What is the goal, the aim of it all? For the Hebrews the aim of education was twofold: The first purpose was the transmission of the historical heritage, the holy story of God's covenant and His workings for His people. They wanted their children to understand that they had an identity—the identity of the people of God. The second aim was instruction in ethical conduct. They wanted their children to know how to conduct their life to attain the utmost happiness on earth. The children were taught to keep the way of the Lord by doing righteousness and dealing justly with others. In simple terms, God's people knew that if a person is to live with others, he must have the holy Other. He must hold God and be held by Him. Is having an identity, and holding a way of life, still important?

A recent C.B.S. special report on teenage murder was horrifying. It was staggering to hear those young men, 15 to 17 years old, speak of why they had killed someone. "That's just how we live," said one. "Their side comes into your territory and you waste them, and you expect the same from them when you go into their territory." Another said, "It's easy, you see, if you got a piece; you just squeeze the trigger. The matter's settled, and you don't have to mess up your clothes." And one more young man said, "I just wanted to see how it felt."

One of the psychologists who worked with the young men in prison, trying to piece it together, made an obvious but perceptive observation: "I don't think we'll ever be able to assess the impact of what our kids see on television. Do you realize that by the time our children are teenagers they see some 15,000 murders on television programs. It's all unreal to them. They become numb and indifferent to it. They are untouched by another's pain."

What is the purpose of our education, our teaching? What is the purpose of it all for the children? Jesus said: "Go therefore and make disciples"—

give them an identity, redeem them, reclaim them. "Baptizing them in the name of the Father and of the Son and of the Holy Spirit"—give them an identity and a way of life with God that they may live life with others. "Teaching them to observe all that I have commanded you"—yes, teach them to guard and keep watch, to hold fast to My way of life; teach them to march to My orders! Yes, baptize, teach and make disciples. . . .

Ultimately in our education we do more than make followers of Christ. True, the word *matheetees,* which we translate "disciple," does mean that; it does mean one who seeks to be an imitator of Christ. Jesus did say that everyone when he is fully taught will be like his teacher. But every disciple soon discovers that his life makes a poor carbon of Christ; his life, at best, draws only a crude and incomplete picture of Jesus. Every disciple soon knows he does not duplicate the depth of Jesus' love and forgiveness and compassion. That is why every disciple learns to be first and foremost a proclaimer of God's love in Jesus Christ.

From Pastor Paul Woundenberg comes this personal parable. He had gone into his garage to discover that 30 or 40 jars, individually and carefully sorted and filled with nuts and nails, bolts and screws, had been dumped in one giant pile on the garage floor by his two daughters. Pastor Woundenberg writes:

> I was furious. I had warned them about it before. So I spanked them properly, and they fled wailing inside. Later little Betsy, blubbery and contrite, came to me and made her way to my lap, melting my anger. Mary, the other daughter, tried to be super-good the rest of the day helping her mother.
>
> There is a parable here: From time to time we mess up God's plan. We know what the rules are, and yet we mix things up. Life goes pretty sick after that. We are not happy. We are off balance. But if we are honest about it, we move to confession. And if a poor mortal daddy can show mercy, certainly God can do much better, even if our sins are a lot bigger. Note carefully that restitution or personal merit has nothing to do with it. My girls cannot help me straighten things out in the garage. And often we aren't able to restore the damage we have caused. But God is merciful to us anyhow.

Yes, in the end that is what a disciple is—a proclaimer of the Christ who has died for me and is risen and will let nothing separate me from the love of God . . . Yes, in the end that is what a disciple is—a proclaimer of the Christ who is Help and Hope, Redeemer and Forgiver. That is the Word that is painted over my life, over my house, over my household, making of it a House of Life.

"You shall therefore lay up these words of mine in your heart and in your soul. . . . You shall teach them to your children. . . . And you shall write them upon the doorposts of your house and upon your gates, that your days and the days of your children may be multiplied in the land which the Lord swore to your fathers to give them, as long as the heavens are above the earth."

Yes, Lord, help me to teach it, to learn it, to live it, to love it, to proclaim it. You are with me always, to the close of the age. Make my home and my heart a House of Life for all Your children.

Daniel A. Benuska

Related Scripture Readings

Deut. 6:4-9, 20-25 Col. 1:9-14; 2:6-7 Matt. 28:16-20

Suggested Hymns

"Shepherd of Tender Youth"
"I am Jesus' Little Lamb"
"You Parents, Hear What Jesus Taught"
"Let Children Hear the Mighty Deeds"
"My Hope Is Built on Nothing Less"

CONFIRMATION

Dare to Be an Andrew

JOHN 1:39-42a; 6:8-9; 12:20-22

It is not unusual for young people of confirmation age to have someone to whom they look up, a so-called hero. They admire this individual and want to do what he or she does and be like this person. Such an individual may be a parent, a teacher, some leading figure in the sporting world, a scientist, or any such prominent, well-known person.

On this blessed, joyful day of your confirmation you are declaring your choice of One whom you would seek to follow in your life. As you affirm the promise made through your sponsors at your baptism, you are saying that you want to be a follower of the Lord Jesus Christ. You want Him to be the Lord and Master of your life as you strive to walk in His ways and to conform your life to His holy will. You are saying that you will believe in Christ and serve Him all your days. This is truly a blessed choice, which, under the guidance of God's Holy Spirit, will give you the full life, the life that will bring you eternal glory.

But what does making such a choice require of you? In declaring that you will be faithful to Christ and serve Him all the days of your life, what are you saying you will do? For your guidance and for help and power in living your life to Christ, I direct your thoughts to the message of our texts.

May the Holy Spirit help us to

Dare to Be an Andrew

If you were asked to name the disciples of Jesus, you probably would not think of Andrew first. We more commonly think of Peter, or John, or even Judas Iscariot. While Andrew is the brother of Simon Peter, he is the more quiet type. We would classify him as an ordinary person, not particularly outstanding. But the Holy Scriptures present him as a true, loyal, and active disciple of the Lord Jesus. And because he is more of an ordinary person, not having special gifts or unusual abilities, we can more readily relate to him. We feel Andrew is a man who speaks our language and lives our kind of life. He is an example whom we feel comfortable in following. To him we now look for lessons we can learn for our life as a follower of Christ.

With a Sincere Faith

In the verses preceding our text in the first chapter of John's gospel, we are told that Andrew was a disciple or follower of John the Baptist. John was the forerunner who pointed to Jesus and declared Him to be "the Lamb of God, who takes away the sin of the world" (John 1:29). Andrew and a companion followed Jesus that day, and we are told "they came and saw where Jesus was staying, and they stayed with Him that day."

As Andrew heard the Gospel declaration of John that this Jesus of Nazareth was the Lamb of God, as he sat with Jesus that day and no doubt heard Jesus speak and teach concerning the purpose of His coming into this world, Andrew was by the gracious working of the Holy Spirit brought to the conviction of a true faith that this Jesus is indeed the promised Savior. His reaction to all he heard that day was that he had found the Messiah. His acceptance of Christ as Lord and Savior was not just a passing fancy but was a genuine acknowledgment that Jesus is truly the Son of God and the promised Savior of the world. In the account of the call of Andrew as told us in the fourth chapter of the Gospel of Matthew, we learn of Andrew's response to Christ's call to discipleship. When Jesus bade them, "Follow Me," Andrew and his brother Peter "left their nets and followed Him" (vv. 19-20). This disciple showed what place he gave Jesus in his life. He made Him the Lord and Master of his life. He was ready to put Christ ahead of even his earthly calling and do His bidding and serve Him. This is a sincere devotion to the Lord and expresses a firm conviction and acceptance of Jesus as his Lord and his God.

Do You Really Believe?

Like Andrew, you too, members of this confirmation class, as well as all of us, have heard the proclamation of the Gospel telling us who Jesus is and of His glorious, saving work. You too have sat at Jesus' feet as you have studied His Word and learned the lessons and truths He teaches us in the Holy Scriptures. Today you are affirming your response to the call of the Savior to be one of His followers. This is a day for all of us, and especially you young people, to search our hearts and to consider what our declaration of faith really means to us. Do you really believe?

This day of your confirmation must be more than just a passing event in your life. It is not simply a ceremony of long tradition that you are asked by your church to participate in, because this is the way we do it in our church. Today you are giving answer to the call to discipleship. What response are you ready to give? What does Christ really mean to you? Let Andrew be your example. May the Holy Spirit have so worked in your heart, that, as you have heard and learned the Gospel message of salvation in Christ Jesus, you too have come to the sincere conviction this Jesus is indeed the very Son of God and the true Son of man. He has taken all your sins upon Himself and has carried them to the cross and there has obtained for you forgiveness, life, and salvation. Believe this with all your heart. This is not the day for form and ceremonies. This is the day for conviction and confession. As you know and accept Jesus as your Savior and your Redeemer, you have the blessed assurance of pardon for all sins from your Father in heaven, the peace of God which surpasses our understanding, and the glorious hope of life with Him that knows no end. Express this confident faith in giving Jesus the first place in your life.

You make many choices in life, the choice of fun and good times, the choice of your life's vocation and calling, the choice of a school for higher education, the choice of a partner or mate with whom you want to share your life. In all of these choices seek first the way and will of your Lord and Master. Let Jesus be always in your thinking and in your planning, in your deciding and in your acting, that your life may express the sincerity of your faith and the genuineness of your confession that you are a follower of Christ.

With a Growing Faith

The disciple Andrew had the blessed privilege of being with Jesus during His earthly ministry and of hearing Him preach and teach the people. What he had come to know and confess about Jesus of Nazareth became even more meaningful to him as he learned ever more deeply to understand these teachings and what they meant for him in his life. We are told in the early part of chapter 13 of the Gospel of Mark how Andrew sought to grow in his faith. In the last days of Christ's earthly ministry, as He spoke to His disciples of the things that were to come, it was Andrew, together with several of his fellow disciples, who asked: "Tell us, when will this be, and what will be the sign when these things are all to be accomplished?" (Mark

13:4). Andrew was a learner, a searcher for truth and understanding. He sought to grow in the faith that was so important to him.

This is a pattern we must follow in our lives as followers of Jesus. Your confirmation today does not mark a point of completion in your Christian life. It is only a step. Do you really understand and fully comprehend all that Christ means to you? Just as in your earthly life you do not completely know what life is all about, so in your life in Christ there is so much more for you to learn and understand. You have the opportunity to grow in faith through your continued use and study of God's Word. Be faithful in your attendance at worship where the messages of God's Word and the truths of the Holy Scriptures are explained and proclaimed. Use the Bible classes provided by your church to grow in your knowledge of God's will and way for your life. Read and study your Bible regularly in your own personal life. You will be joyfully surprised how even familiar truths will open up for you in a new meaning. As your depth of knowledge grows and your comprehension of Bible truths deepens, the Word of God will be more and more a treasure for you in your life, and your faith in Christ will become richer and more meaningful. Then you will be heeding the admonition of Andrew's brother Peter: "Grow in the grace and knowledge of our Lord and Savior Jesus Christ" (2 Peter 3:18). May the Holy Spirit increase your faith, so that it becomes ever more a joy and a blessing, a comfort and a power in your life.

With an Active Faith

Such a genuine and sincere faith also expresses itself in action. Andrew is an example for us in this respect, as shown in the familiar incident of the feeding of the five thousand. We read in our text: "Andrew, Simon Peter's brother, said to Jesus, 'There is a lad here who has five barley loaves and two fish; but what are they among so many?' " Jesus had asked the disciples how they might provide food so the multitude could eat. They were perplexed, not knowing what to do. But Andrew looked around, trying to see if there was some way he could help. He found this young boy with the fish and bread. It was a little thing, but he was trying to help, trying to serve his Master. When Andrew found the boy with the small portion of food, he wondered if that would do any good. But he left that up to Jesus. We know what the almighty Savior did with the five loaves and the two fish. And it was all because Andrew showed his trust and reliance on the Lord. His faith and confidence would not sit back and give up. His faith expressed itself, and he became a helper in making possible Christ's wonderful miracle of feeding the five thousand.

As we live our lives as Christ's followers, this is something for us to remember. Little things can become great with Jesus. There are times when we may want to help, but we feel that what we may be able to do does not really count. We are thinking only of our own abilities and efforts and forgetting that Jesus can accomplish great things even with little. As Christians, we are called upon to use whatever opportunities we have, as little as they might seem, to express our trust and reliance on our Lord and Savior. You are not too young, too limited in ability, too unimportant to be a helper for Christ. Let your faith show. Seek to serve. Be a helper in whatever way you can. When you see a person who needs help and you can provide that help, do it. When you have a service you can give—at home, at school, in your work—give that service to the best of your ability, willingly, with joy in being able to serve your Lord. People cannot see the faith and trust in your heart, but they can see that faith as it works in acts of love and helpfulness. Little do we know what blessings Christ can bring through us to others as we live our faith and let it work for Him.

With a Shared Faith

One of the wonderful ways we can show our faith is by sharing it with others. This was almost the spontaneous response of Andrew's faith when he found the Messiah. Our text tells us that when Andrew came to the knowledge that Jesus is the Messiah, "He first found his brother Simon, and said to him, 'We have found the Messiah.' " This knowledge was so great, this news was so wonderful, that Andrew could not keep it to himself. He had to share the faith that had come to him, and he sought out his brother so that he too might experience the joy of faith. Later in his days with Jesus we are told in our text: "Now among those who went up to worship at the feast were some Greeks. So these came to Philip, who was from Bethsaida in Galilee, and said to him, 'Sir, we wish to see Jesus'. Philip went and told Andrew; Andrew went with Philip and they told Jesus." It was Andrew who was sought out when the opportunity arose to bring others to Jesus. He would be a messenger for Christ. He was so filled with the joy and hope of his faith in the Savior that he willingly and readily shared it with others.

This is a privilege all of us enjoy. It is a way we can express the meaning of our faith in our lives. Your confirmation today is not a private or secret ceremony. You are openly declaring that Jesus is your Life and your Salvation. Never be ashamed of that confession. You need to pause regularly and consider what Jesus means to you. Though you falter and go astray, you know that in the mercy and grace of Jesus you have forgiveness. When you are troubled and carrying burdens in your life, you know that you have the almighty and ever-present Lord to be with you and to strengthen and help you. When you are sad and downcast, Jesus comforts you with the assurance: "I will never fail you nor forsake you" (Heb. 13:5). When everything around you seems to fall and tumble, you have the faith that overcomes the world. In Christ you have the one and only way that leads to the blessed victory of life everlasting. This, by the grace of God, is your faith. This is the treasure you acclaim in your confession today.

Now this is so good, so wonderful, so meaningful, that you must not keep it to yourself. Speak of your faith. Share it with others. As you associate with others at home, at school, in your work, in your neighborhood, let people see Christ in your speech and in your actions. Even when others around you may not agree or are indifferent toward the church and religion, don't clam up. Speak up, let others know the joy and trust you have in Jesus. At a McDonald's restaurant three Lutheran girls were employed. After about four months the manager of that restaurant started to attend their church and a short time later joined the adult instruction class. He stated that his reason for that decision was these three girls. As he observed the way they went about their work, their conversation, their friendliness and general attitude, he said that was the kind of life he wanted; he wanted the faith they expressed in their lives. In your speech, in your conduct, in your whole way of life you can be witnesses for Jesus, you can be another Andrew. You, and all of us, do well today and often to ask ourselves if our lives, our words and actions, give testimony of Jesus' love and power.

As you today make your confession that you are a follower of Jesus, as all of us renew that vow for ourselves, may we often look to the apostle Andrew and learn from him what is required of us as Christ's disciples. Be steadfast and firm in your faith. Grow in your conviction and trust in Christ. May that faith be alive and active in your life so that as others observe you in your daily living they will recognize that you have been with Jesus. Amen.

Edgar C. Rakow

Related Scripture Readings

2 Kings 5:2-8
Ps. 25:1-7
Is. 43:1-3a, 10-13
Matt. 4:18-25
John 15:1-8
Col. 3:12-17
1 John 1:1-7

Suggested Hymns

"Jesus Calls Us"
"Speak, O Lord, Thy Servant Heareth"
"Baptized into Thy Name Most Holy"
"Let Me Be Thine Forever"
"Jesus, Jesus, Only Jesus"
"Jesus Christ, My Pride and Glory"
"Spread, Oh, Spread, Thou Mighty Word"
"I Love to Tell the Story"

DEDICATION OF A CHURCH BUILDING

What Is a House of God?

GEN. 28:17

To gather in this new house of God is a joyous occasion. For some it gives a sense of accomplishment—after years of planning, of gathering funds, of being in a temporary place of worship, of sacrifice and giving. Its very appearance is beautiful to behold, in all its newness and with all its niceties. In these spacious accommodations so much can be done for God's children! His Word, His sacraments can come to His people, so they might all have assurance of forgiveness of sins, resurrection of the body, and life everlasting. Just the joys of accomplishment, of appearance, and of the accommodations are enough to cause us to praise God again and again.

Let's go back to the words of reaction which another child of God gave when, while running away to save his life, he awoke one morning assured of God's grace and presence.

Jacob was on his way to visit Uncle Laban. He lay down to sleep, and in his sleep dreamed that there was a ladder of steps going from earth to heaven, with angels ascending and descending on that ladder. Standing by Jacob was the Lord Himself, who said: "I am the Lord, the God of Abraham and Isaac. I will give to you and your descendants this land on which you are lying. They will be as numerous as the specks of dust on the earth. They will extend their territory in all directions, and through you and your descendants I will bless all the nations. Remember, I will be with you and protect you wherever you go, and I will bring you back to this land. I will not leave you until I have done all that I have promised you" (Gen. 28:13-15 TEV).

When Jacob awoke from his sleep he recognized that indeed God would be with him, and for the joy of that memory he vowed to return again and to dedicate his life more and more to his Lord. He called the name of that place "Bethel," which means "House of God," for he said: "This is none other than the house of God, and this is the gate of heaven" (RSV).

What Is a House of God?

I. A Place of Rest

What then is a "house of God"? What then is this place, which you dedicate today to God's glory, the place for which you have worked so hard?

What is a house of God? Is it not a place of rest, just as it was for Jacob? After a long and weary journey, Jacob found it to be a place where he had found rest. As we do, Jacob had many problems. He had lied to his father. He had connived to trick his brother, Esau. He had been involved with his mother so that he might make the deal to obtain what belonged to another. His name meant "wrestler" or "trickster," and it seemed that so he was appropriately named. He ran away from home and no more could find joy or peace there.

He was tired, and eventide was at hand. He would lie down to rest. For him the place was a place of rest, "the house of God, the gate of heaven."

The Lord has encouraged us to remember a day wherein we, too, can rest. That's what the Hebrew word "sabbath" means, "rest." It is here in this place where we find rest. The Lord of the church speaks to us to gather here and find rest for our souls, we who are weary and heavy laden. As it says in Psalm 127, "He gives to His beloved sleep." He is not referring to sleeping during the sermon, of course. But as we come here, tired and weary from our journeys, as we come here victims or victors in certain trickeries of life, as we come here because of greed that disturbs or mistakes that plague us in life, we too want to find rest. You come here with your burdens and pains—burdens too heavy to bear, hearts breaking because of grief, anxieties and worries weakening our lives, loneliness making us cry out for love. We come into this house of God to find rest for our souls.

And what is that rest? It is that the angels of Christmas tell us that we need not be afraid, for a Savior has been born for us, One to take away our sins. We hear the announcement and word of the angels at our side, declaring: "He is risen from the dead." Death has been conquered for us and all mankind. As Jesus said so often, angels will be "ascending and descending upon the Son of Man" (John 1:51) and there will be that great judgment day when our Savior will be on His throne, and the angels as reapers will come to gather us into His eternal home. And because we have been in the house of God and heard His words of assurance in Word and sacrament, we can rejoice in forgiveness of sins, resurrection of the body, and life everlasting. This is the House of God to give unto us rest.

II. A Place of Revelation

What then is a "house of God"? A place of rest, and yet more; it is a place of revelation.

Archaeologists tell us that the steeps and steps of the rocks at the place where Jacob lay down to rest could easily have been an old-fashioned ziggurat, that is, a temple which people had built in step-fashion in order to get closer to God. Such temples still are to be found in Mexico.

And so, as Jacob lies down to sleep by this old temple, this old place where men wanted to draw near to God, and the angels came down and ascended, Jacob found the true God, the Lord Himself, Jehovah, who was the God of Abraham and the God of Isaac, and who also would covenant to be the God of Jacob. And thus Jacob could rise to praise God and say that this was the house of the LORD God, the God of all gods.

This is a church. Is it like any other building? No, this building is the house of the Lord, for here will be proclaimed and given the revelation of God's full and total Word. This house is dedicated to have the congregation assemble and hear the Word of God proclaimed by the pastor—week after week; in season, out of season; year in, year out. Here will be shared the treasures of God's wisdom from the revelation of His will according to the Law, calling us to know God's will, calling us to repent of wrongs against His will, and reminding us again and again of His judgment. But even more this house of the Lord will resound and echo with the good news of the glorious Gospel of the blessed God, as we will hear revealed unto us over and over the grace of God, the good news of God's love to us, in that He became flesh and dwelt among us, was crucified for our sins, and was raised again for our justification.

Here our children, and those of other folks, will be brought to the healing waters of Holy Baptism, that they might be born again into His kingdom, buried with Christ in God's gracious washing so they might rise again to newness of life.

And as those who are instructed and have become partners in this great community of faith, they will stand around the table, partake of the bread and wine, and in it and with it receive the body and blood of Jesus Christ for the assurance of forgiveness and of life everlasting.

Thus you come into this house of God, seeking rest, and find the revelation from on high. Thus was Jacob reassured at the place he called Bethel—the house of God.

There he found revealed God's abiding presence. As a fish does not say to the water, "Please get closer to me"; as a bird does not say to the air, "Please get closer to me"; so a child of God need not cry out, "Please get closer to me." For God is present, wherever two or three are gathered in His name. God is present wherever we go in life, but especially when we come here to listen to His Word and rejoice in His presence in our midst. He is at our side to crush the power of the evil ones, the powers of all forces against us, to work all things together for our good.

All the promises of God are here for us—in this place of rest and place of revelation.

III. A Place of Response

When Jacob awoke from the dream and found that joy, he responded that indeed this was the house of God and the gate of heaven. He took oil, poured it on the stone which he had turned upright to be a pillar or monument, and anointed that stone, saying: "This is . . . the house of God." And he made a vow that he would return there and would offer to God thankofferings and gifts for God's love to him.

As you leave this house of God and go on your journey, you too, as he, can go in peace, knowing of God's confidence and grace. Back to the typewriter in the office, to the diapers in the baby's room, to the machines, to the tilling of the soil, to the assembly line, to driving the bus—holding your head high because you know God loves you and cares for you, protects you and guides you; you know of His grace and goodness in Jesus Christ.

All your friends and neighbors today rejoice with you. Your church and its District and Synod are delighted and rejoice with you that you now have this place of worship, this house of God, this gate of heaven. We pray and hope that you will indeed find that this is the place for you and you will come here often—for rest, for His revelation, and for your response to His goodness.

George W. Bornemann

Parallel Scripture Readings

1 Kings 8:1-13	Ps. 100	1 Cor. 3:11-23
1 Kings 8:22-30	Ps. 122	Heb. 10:19-25
Ezra 2:68-69	Luke 19:1-10	1 Peter 2:1-9
Ps. 24	John 2:13-22	Rev. 21:1-5
Ps. 84	John 10:22-30	

Suggested Hymns

"Built on the Rock, the Church Shall Stand"
"Great Is the Lord, Our God
"For Many Years, O God of Grace"
"God the Father, Son, and Spirit"
"I Love Thy Kingdom, Lord"
"The Church's One Foundation"
"Oh, Worship the King, All Glorious Above"

EVANGELISM

Celebrate the Mission

LUKE 24:47

Let's begin our message with a surprise test—pretend, of course. Imagine that you have paper and pencil in hand, and the test is before you. This test has only one question. Here it is: "What is the reason for the existence of the church?" or very simply, "What is the business of the church?"

How would *you* answer that question? We have asked that question many times and have received many answers—"to preach the Gospel," "to save sinners," "to feed the lambs and sheep," "well, we've certainly put a lot of work into this place and it would be a shame to see it all go down the drain," and "well, somebody around here has to take care of all the Lutherans" are some of them. How *would* you answer that question?

Fortunately, we can go directly to Scripture to find the reason for the church's existence. Jesus Himself gave the direction—in unmistakable terms. He did it at least four times, recorded for us at the close of the four gospels. In Matt. 28:18-20 He gave us what we generally call the Great Commission, telling us that our big job is to make disciples of all nations by going, by baptizing, and by teaching. In Mark 16:15 He told us that we are to go into all the world to preach the Gospel, and in John 20:21 He gave us our task in yet other words, saying: "As the Father has sent Me, even so I send you."

Our text is a fourth record of Christ's commissioning word. But let us first put our text into its context! Jesus is speaking to His disciples following His resurrection and His appearance to the two disciples on the Emmaus road. These two disciples had rejoined the rest of the disciples in Jerusalem (Luke 24:33) and shared all the exciting news of that encounter with the risen Lord. As they were sharing, Jesus appeared to all of them. In the midst of their amazement, abiding unbelief, and small understanding, He opened their understanding of the Scriptures (v. 45) by rehearsing for them one more time the purpose of His coming, of His suffering, and the promise of His rising—all that the Scriptures might be fulfilled in demonstration of the great love of God for mankind, and in fulfillment of His redemptive promises in Christ.

Having said all of this, He declared in the words of our text that "repentance and forgiveness of sins should be preached in His name to all nations, beginning from Jerusalem" (Luke 24:47 RSV). With these words Jesus gives the reason for the existence of the church today, for while He spoke these words to the disciples of His day, they are also applicable to us, the disciples of our day. Knowing what we are to do, we can **Celebrate the Mission** that our blessed Lord has given us to do. We can get right on with the task. Let's examine that task, rejoicing in the fact that He has called us to be His colaborers in bringing people into God's family.

I. ". . . in His Name"

Let us first lift from the text the little phrase "in His name." That was an important phrase for the disciples, as it should be for us. The *name* of God, Jahweh, Jehovah, was that by which the children of God knew Him. The name of God was the embodiment of all that God was to the people. It was the summation of all of God's being and teaching. Speaking to Moses, God had said: "Say this to the people of Israel, 'The Lord, the God of your fathers, the God of Abraham, the God of Issac, and the God of Jacob, has sent me to you': this is My name forever, and thus I am to be remembered throughout all generations" (Ex. 3:15 RSV). The psalmist caught this theme, and the importance of the Lord's name, in many psalms, like 113:2: "Blessed be the name of the Lord from this time forth and for evermore." Already in the Ten Commandments God said: "You shall not take the name of the Lord your God in vain; for the Lord will not hold him guiltless who takes His name in vain" (Ex. 20:7).

It must have been little less than shocking to the disciples to hear from the lips of the risen Lord that now all that they were to do was to be done in the name of Jesus. He who was given the name of Jesus because He would save His people from their sins (Matt. 1:21) is now declaring: My name is the name by which salvation is assured; through My name you become right with My heavenly Father.

Today, what we do we must do in the name of Jesus. His name gives authority to our ministry, for he claimed that "all authority in heaven and on earth has been given to Me" (Matt. 28:18). When we minister "in His name" we are simply drawing on that power which is His, and becomes the authority and power by which we minister.

To picture it another way: Suppose that you listed all the ministry of the congregation on paper—things like worship, teaching, fellowship, Christian service to the community, life within the various organizations of the parish—and handed that list to Jesus, *would He give His approval? Would He affix His signature to authenticate what is being done?*

We have to ask ourselves again and again, "Is what we are doing in the church today what Jesus wants us to do? Or are we sometimes simply engaged in busywork, in playing games called 'church,' without getting down to the bedrock mission we are to be doing in the name of Jesus?" If we can assure ourselves that we are on track in what we are doing, then certainly we can celebrate the mission.

II. ". . . Repentance and Forgiveness of Sins Should Be Preached"

Jesus says that we are to be about the business of preaching, of proclaiming repentance and forgiveness. That has always been the burden of the church's message: turn from your sins, and be assured of the redemptive action of a loving God. The ancient prophets all sang the same refrain in their word of judgment and hope to the children of Israel. Jesus is their echo, except that now the message is to be preached in His name.

It's still the same today. All need to hear that word of the need for repentance, and the joyful word of forgiveness. Let's make it very, very personal. Of each of *us* it has been said that we were born dead in trespasses and sins (Eph. 2:1), were born flesh of flesh (John 3:6); have gone astray (Is. 53:6), and were lost (Luke 19:10). Indeed, in our deadness, we were totally unable to save ourselves, except by the grace of God, by which we have been saved through faith (Eph. 2:8-9).

In his condition man needs to hear the word of the Lord as reported through the prophet (Joel 2:12): " 'Yet even now,' says the Lord, 'return to Me with all your heart, with fasting, with weeping, and with mourning; and rend your hearts and not your garments' "; or the word of Jesus Himself, recorded in Luke 13:23, and spoken in reference to Galileans who suffered death at the hand of Pilate: "Do you think that these Galileans were worse sinners . . . because they suffered thus? I tell you, No; but unless you repent you will all likewise perish."

And should any of us think that we have arrived, that we have no sins of which to repent and have no more tears to shed, listen to Paul, who declares to the Philippians that he was not yet perfect (Phil. 3:12) and to the Romans (7:19) that he did not yet do the good he wanted to do, nor did he refrain from doing what he did not want to do. In his struggle he cries out, "Who will deliver me?" (Rom. 7:24), but almost in the next breath he exclaims that deliverance is through Jesus Christ our Lord!

What a message to us who daily stand in need of repentance. In turn our message to others is the same that we ourselves daily need to receive: Repent; turn from your evil way and live; there is forgiveness.

How we rejoice, then, to note that Jesus has a wonderful word for the repentant sinner—the word of forgiveness. Thats what it's all about. That's what Jesus came to do: to offer forgiveness to the repentant, believing sinner. That's His message to the world, to the church, to you and to me. That's the same message we proclaim in His name as our mission to each other and the world. "In Christ God was reconciling the world to Himself" (2 Cor. 5:19)—that's the good Word, the Good News, the Gospel for each of us, for He has redeemed us by His holy, precious blood and His innocent suffering and death. Praise be to His name! And now He calls us into His mission to share in the good work of proclaiming the Word of repentance and the beautiful Word of forgiveness. What a mission to celebrate! What a work to be about!

III. ". . . to All Nations"

This great work is not to be restricted to a few, or to one location. Listen to the word of the text one more time as Jesus says that this word is to be proclaimed to all nations. What this means, of course is that we need a world view, even as our loving Father had when He sent His Son. Remember those many passages from Scripture which attest to the heavenly Father's love for all human beings: "For God so loved the world," (John 3:16), "God was in Christ reconciling the world to Himself" (2 Cor. 5:19), God desires all men to be saved and to come to the knowledge of the truth" (2 Tim. 2:4).

That world view should prompt us to reflect on this, that what the world needs to hear is not that there is a better mouse trap; not that there is a cure to all man's social ills; that the day will come when all will have equal opportunity; that there will always be enough energy for all; that the environment will someday be safe for all in all circumstances; that there is a "sure-fire" way to assure and insure the benefits from Social Security whenever anybody reaches the age of retirement. More than that what the world needs to hear is that there is forgiveness in the atoning blood of the Lamb, that forgiveness has been procured, that redemption is being proclaimed through the grace of God by the people of God to all of God's created people.

It's probably only when we begin to sense the world quality of the Savior's redemptive act that we can begin to understand the vastness of the task before us to bring this good Word to "all nations." Of course, we cannot all go to all places in the world. But we can send our ambassadors, missionaries who go in our place, and in our stead proclaim the good Word about repentance and the joyful Word of forgiveness. In The Lutheran Church—Missouri Synod, all of us in some 6,000 congregations support the cause of the Lord's mission by sending missionaries where we cannot go. In our stead some 160 American missionaries are working in about 22 countries of the world; additionally we help support national pastors and churches in many of these countries. Add to that support of the Lutheran Hour and other agencies which bring the same word of truth to the whole world—and we have a mission to celebrate. What joy to be on target for the Lord!

IV. ". . . Beginning at Jerusalem"

There is just one phrase of our text left! Jesus says that this Word of repentance and forgiveness is to be proclaimed to all nations, *beginning at Jerusalem*.

Would you join me in acknowledging that speaking the Word of repentance and forgiveness in our Jerusalem is often the hardest part of our mission? It's easier at times to put folding money into a mission envelope and feel that we have been part of a sending church than to speak to the man next door, or to members of our own family. How many times do we witness to each other? Husbands to wives? Wives to husbands? Parents to children? Brothers to sisters? Is it not true that our own private little Jerusalem can be void of testimony to the great forgiveness we share in Christ Jesus? And yet, that's where Jesus says it is to begin.

Merton P. Strommen in *A Study of Generations,* a study about the habits of Lutherans, concludes that 50% of all Lutherans do no witnessing at all, 40% witness sometimes, and only 10% do considerable witnessing, like giving somebody a tract, speaking of their faith to somebody, making a visit, inviting people to church, and so forth. If that is true, what a pity!

Further, studies conducted by the Institute for American Church Growth indicate that up to 80% of people who join a church were first introduced to the church by a relative, friend, or acquaintance. If this is true, what a challenge to each of us to begin working in our own Jerusalem, by speaking a word of forgiveness or repentance to some of the eight people we are said to have in our circle of acquaintances to whom we could each bring good positive witness. What celebrating of mission if each of us would begin by just reaching out to *one* in that circle of friends, relatives, or acquaintances!

On a recent trip to New York I had occasion to travel some of the many freeways. Imagine my surprise when I saw emblazoned in bold letters on the gymnasium of a very large Roman Catholic parish these words: EACH ONE REACH ONE. How quickly my mind turned to our Lutheran Church—Missouri Synod effort of a generation ago when that same slogan encouraged each of us to begin in our own little Jerusalem. That's where it begins. Thats where Jesus says it begins.

Of course, to those of us who say that we do not know how to begin to witness in our own Jerusalem, He also speaks a good word as He promises the power of His Holy Spirit. To His disciples He gave the promise that even in the face of persecution they need have no fear about what they should say, because He said that "what you are to say will be given you in that hour; for it is not you who speak, but the Spirit of your Father speaking through you" (Matt. 10:19b-20). That's indeed comforting—and cause for celebration!

The good news is that more and more people—through encouragement from the Word of God, through encouragement from each other, through training in witnessing and evangelizing, and through the discovery of the joy of witnessing by the power of the Spirit—are engaged in and are excited about being on the Lord's mission, and celebrate it regularly.

But if we don't? Let me share a little story I read years ago. It deals with World War II and the bombings of Germany. In some city, one of the great cathedrals was inadvertently struck and demolished. After the bombing, parishioners sifted through the ruins to see what could be salvaged from their beautiful temple. Imagine their surprise when they came upon the life-size statue of Christ lying amidst the rubble and the tangled mass of beams and dust—unscratched, except that in the forward fall from the high altar, both uplifted hands had been snapped off right at the wrists.

What to do with the statue? Many hours of dialog led to a decision that can be noted today. As you walk into the rebuilt cathedral, there in the narthex stands the same statue, unscratched, arms uplifted, hands missing. Underneath, for all who walk by, is an arresting inscription. It says simply: YOU ARE MY HANDS.

And that's the way it is. He has no other hands to do His work; no other feet to run His messages; no other lips to sing His praise—but ours.

How great therefore to be in service to and with Him, to be in mission as He has directed, to be honestly celebrating what you do for Him because what you are doing is what He wants you to do!

To God be the glory!

W. Leroy Biesenthal

Related Scripture Readings

Mal. 3:16-18 Matt. 4:18-25 Eph. 2:1-10

Suggested Hymns

"Today Thy Mercy Calls Us"
"The Gospel Shows the Father's Grace"
"The Law of God Is Good and Wise"
"Jesus! and Shall It Ever Be"
"Thou Art the Way; to Thee Alone"
"O Jesus, King Most Wonderful"
"By Grace I'm Saved, Grace Free and Boundless"
"Jesus Shall Reign Where'er the Sun"

FATHER'S DAY

Our Father and Our Fathers

LUKE 11:1-2a

Mrs. John Bruce Dodd of Spokane, Wash., started Father's Day in 1910, but it wasn't until 1936 that a National Father's Day Committee was formed. I am in favor of a Father's Day, but probably for a different reason than most fathers. As a pastor, Father's Day gives me an occasion to remind us fathers of our God-given responsibilities. Being a Christian father or mother goes beyond the natural instincts we possess, which cause us to care for the babies we help produce; and not everything we have learned from observation of other parents should be copied in our parenting. So I think we need a Father's Day not so much to thank and praise our fathers but to help us remember what God expects of the fathers.

Our theme today as we base our message on the introduction of the Lord's Prayer is:

Our Father and Our Fathers

We can learn much about both from Jesus. James Tissot, the French Biblical illustrator, pictured Jesus seated on the Mount of Olives with His disciples when they asked, "Lord, teach us to pray, as John taught his disciples." Perhaps John had taught his disciples that prayer could be used for petitions, that is, to ask God for what is needed, rather than exclusively to praise God, and Jesus' disciples wanted to know if this was a correct use of prayer. Jesus' discourse on prayer in Luke 11, with His emphases on "ask, seek, and knock," plus His two illustrations, make it clear that they should indeed use prayer to request. But more important than the purpose of prayer for our concern is how to address God.

In His Sermon on the Mount and again on this occasion, Jesus said, "When you pray, say: 'Our Father' " (KJV). Jesus teaches us to address God in prayer not as "Jehovah," "God," "Lord," or "Almighty One," but as "Father." The terms "Lord" or "God" remind us of His sovereignty; the term "Father," however, shows us His grace, love, kindness, mercy, nearness, and intimacy.

"Father" is the term Jesus used to indicate His own intimate relationship with God. The first recorded words of Christ are Luke 2:49, where the 12-year-old Jesus asked His mother: "How is it that you sought Me? Did you not know that I must be in My Father's house?" (RSV). Or, as the King James version has, "about my Father's business?" The Greek suggests this translation: "Didn't you know I had to be at My Father's?" It's like a child announcing as he goes out the door, "I'll be at Johnnie's." This I believe is what astonished the doctors—not only that He was a 12-year-old boy with a knowledge of Scripture far beyond His years, but His intimate way of talking about God.

Have you ever tried to call the President of the United States on your telephone? Even if you made it a person-to-person call to President Reagan, there is no way that you could talk to him. You would get no farther than to an aide or secretary. The President has to be protected from people making crank calls or asking big favors, so he has a huge staff of people handling the calls that come into the White House, and these people direct the calls to others beside the President. There are four people, however, who can call the White House and be put right through to the President himself. These four people are Maureen (born in 1941), Michael (born in 1946), Patricia (born in 1953), and Ronald (born in 1959). They can get through because they call the President "Father."

Jesus had immediate access to God because He called God "Father," and now He invites His followers to address God as their father too. I read a story about a college student from a wealthy family who had a roommate who was a very poor boy. The rich student took the poor one home with him for a weekend and said, "Don't call my father 'Sir' or 'Mr.'; call him 'Dad' and ask for anything you want, and he'll give to you because you are my friend."

This is what Jesus is conveying when He says: "When you pray say, Our Father" (KJV). Luther reminds us in his Small Catechism: "God would by these words tenderly invite us to believe that He is our true Father, and that we are His true children, so that we may with all boldness and confidence ask Him as dear children ask their dear father."

God is our Father because He redeemed us in and through Jesus Christ. In Gal. 4:4-5 (RSV) we are told: "When the time had fully come, God sent forth His Son, born of woman, born under the Law, to redeem those who were under the Law, so that we might receive adoption as sons." True, our sins had separated us from our Father, but in Christ we have been brought together again.

Paul writes in Rom. 8:14-17 (RSV): "For all who are led by the Spirit of God are sons of God. . . . You have received the spirit of sonship. When we cry, 'ABBA! FATHER!' it is the Spirit Himself bearing witness with our spirit that we are children of God, and if children, then heirs, heirs of God and fellow heirs with Christ."

II. Our Fathers

Because today is "Father's Day," let's now take a look at our other father, for it is the picture of a human father that Jesus wants us to have when we address God as "Father." The human fathers have their day today, but I'm not so concerned about how children are to honor their fathers as how fathers are to act toward their offspring.

I reviewed all the recorded words of Jesus in the gospels and noted all the times He talked not only about the heavenly Father but about earthly fathers. From Jesus' words there develops an ideal father pictured by our Lord. The ideal father is one who is a pattern, a provider, a protector, a prophet, and a priest for his family.

First, it was obvious to Jesus that the father is a pattern to be copied by his children. He said in John 8:19: "If you knew Me, you would know My Father also." He also said in verse 41: "You do what your father did." In verse 39 He said: "If you were Abraham's children, you would do what Abraham did." And in verse 44: "You are of your father the devil, and your will is to do your father's desires."

Jesus' way of contrasting the works of Abraham and the devil is a stinging reminder needed today. Fathers, children still do the deeds of their fathers. You are their pattern whether you want to be or not. Your attitude toward God, His name, His Word, His worship will be reflected in your children. A study made of U. S. soldiers during the Vietnam War years indicated that 75% of those whose fathers attended church were still with the church; but regardless of the mother's worship practice, when fathers stayed home, three of four sons dropped out too, in their early teens. Authorities report that runaway children pour out to them stories of what they have run away from: fathers who are drunkards, immoral, cheaters, child and wife abusers. Fathers, we have been entrusted with a great responsibility. We are called upon to live in such a way and to lead in such a way that in us our children are enabled to see Christ and our heavenly Father.

Youngsters are not likely to run away from fathers they admire or from a place where they feel loved. Fathers who worship regularly usually have children who do the same. Generosity begets generosity, love produces love. Fathers, let the loving pattern the Lord has revealed to us cause you to be the best kind of pattern you can be for your children so that when someone reminds your son he resembles his dad he sticks out his chest, not his tongue.

Second, Jesus calls upon a father to be a provider. He asks in this chapter on prayer, verses 11 to 13: "What father among you, if his son asks for a fish, will instead give him a serpent; or if he asks for an egg, will give him a scorpion? If you then, who are evil, know how to give good gifts to your children, how much more will the heavenly Father give the Holy Spirit to those who ask Him!"

Luther reminds us of God giving good gifts in his explanation of the First Article of the Apostles' Creed: "He provides me with food and clothing, home and family, daily work, and all I need from day to day. . . . All this He does out of fatherly and divine goodness and mercy, though I do not deserve it" *(The Small Catechism in Contemporary English).*

Thus God sets a splendid example for us to follow in providing for those entrusted to us. Fathers are to provide what children need in order to grow in four ways: spiritually, physically, emotionally, and mentally. As unthinkable as it is for even an evil father to give a snake for a fish, or a scorpion for an egg to his children, how much more will a divinely motivated father give the good gifts of Word and sacrament, health care, social opportunities, and a good education to his children.

Third, Jesus reveals that a father is a protector. When, in the story immediately following the Lord's Prayer in Luke's prayer chapter, an unexpected visitor caused a neighbor to wake up a father to ask for bread, the father's excuse was, "My children are with me in bed; I cannot get up and give you anything" (v. 7).

In three of Jesus' miracles fathers are rewarded for their faith and loving concern for their children. One was Jairus, who was a ruler of the synagogue and yet fell down at Jesus' feet and begged Him to come to his house because his only daughter was dying (Luke 8:41 ff.). The second was a nobleman from Capernaum who went to Jesus and begged Him to come down and heal his son, for he was at the point of death (John 4:46 ff.). The third was a father who brought his son who was possessed by a demon while Jesus was on the mountain of transfiguration. The disciples were unable to heal the son, so when Jesus came down the father pleaded for healing for his son (Matt. 17:14 ff.).

Good fathers protect their children from physical and spiritual harm. They teach their children how to defend their faith and their lives.

A fourth role of a father as shown by the Lord is that of prophet. In the Old Testament, God commanded the fathers to teach His will and His commandments to their children, and most of the teaching was done by word of mouth as it was passed down from father to son. Mothers and younger children stayed home, but fathers and their older sons went to

Jerusalem for the three weeklong feasts. At Jerusalem the fathers were taught the word of Scripture in continuing postgraduate courses so that they could go home and conduct family devotions. In John 17:8 Jesus said to the Father in prayer: "I have given them the words which Thou gavest Me, and they have received them."

Following His resurrection, the Lord gave the church the continuation of this task by saying: "Feed My lambs" (John 21:15). Faithful fathers take the lead in family devotions, in getting the family to church, and seeing their children are taught the Word of God.

Finally, the fifth role of a father is that of priest. A priest is one who pleads to God for others. The best example I can find in the Bible of a father serving as a priest for his children is Job of the Old Testament. We are told in Job 1:5 that he would rise up early in the morning and offer burnt offerings according to the number of his seven sons and three daughters, for he said, "It may be that my sons have sinned, and cursed God in their hearts."

A good father will pray daily for his children's salvation. Jesus set the example. In His prayer at the end of His life He prayed to the Father: "I am praying for them. I am not praying for the world but for those whom Thou hast given Me, for they are Thine" (John 17:9).

The picture is that we parents are caretakers of the children God entrusts to us and we will one day have to give an accounting to God of our stewardship of these children. Some will be lost in spite of all the love and care they received. Even Jesus had to admit in His high-priestly prayer: "Those that Thou gavest Me I have kept, and none of them is lost but the son of perdition" (John 17:12 KJV). We all know of a son or daughter who turned away from parents and the heavenly Father in spite of everything being done that parents should do. They grieve for their children as David did for Absalom or Jesus did for Judas, whom He calls "the son of perdition." Let it not be said that we led them astray. What a joy, however, to report: "Those that Thou gavest Me I have kept, and none of them is lost" (KJV).

In conclusion let me say that the encyclopedia defines "father" as a title of respect and honor given to men who establish anything important in human affairs. Thus George Washington is called the father of our nation, Hippocrates is called the father of medicine, James Madison is called the father of the constitution. The father of angling is Izaak Walton, who wrote about the delights of fishing in 1653.

It is indeed an honor that we can address God as "Our Father," and we fathers would do well to make our Father our example. Amen.

Elmer E. Scheck

Related Scripture Readings

Matt. 7:7-12 Matt. 15:3-9 Eph. 6:1-4

Suggested Hymns

"God of Our Fathers"
"Faith of Our Fathers"
"For All the Saints Who from Their Labors Rest"
"O Blessed Home Where Man and Wife"

FUNERAL

Christian Confidence in the Face of Death

2 TIM. 4:6-8

"Come, sweet death!"

These words might well have been in the heart of this man last Friday evening. At the close of a few days' leave from the hospital, he asked for the pastor to come for a devotion with the family. Then, saying to the children: "Take care of your mother, and don't ever forget Jesus," he turned his wheelchair to leave home and return to the hospital. He knew what lay ahead. There was no wavering, no uncertainty. Within 12 hours he was dead, a victim of cancer.

It had been a long illness, and there were a few times, very few, when he grew weary and experienced some discouragement. Like the people of Israel, when they had to take a long, circuitous route through the desert on the way to the Promised Land—the Scriptures say of them: "The soul of the people was much discouraged because of [the rigors of] the way" (Num. 21:4 KJV).

There were rigors for Paul L——————, sometimes intense suffering. As long as medical science held out a bit of hope, he held on with a firm hand. We wondered at times how he could continue to hold on, but he bore the load without complaint. But when the message got through that there was no hope for reversing the ravages of the disease, he turned to face his death—with certainty, with assurance, with full acceptance, knowing that he would not face this enemy alone, but would go through it with his Savior at his side.

It was this full-of-faith attitude that moved us to select these words of Scripture for this service, the words found in 2 Tim. 4:6-8: "I am already on the point of being sacrificed; the time of my departure has come. I have fought the good fight, I have finished the race, I have kept the faith. Henceforth there is laid up for me the crown of righteousness, which the Lord, the righteous Judge, will award to me on that Day, and not only to me but also to all who have loved His appearing."

I

These words were written by another Paul to the young preacher Timothy at Ephesus. Paul the apostle was in prison in Rome at the time. He had been there once before, spending two years in prison at Caesarea and then two more in Rome before he was released. When he was discharged he went back to work, but for only a brief time. He was arrested a second time. We are not given the details, and the tradition about the situation is unclear, but Paul knew what was going to happen. This time there would be no escape. Evidently execution by beheading was only a short time away. That's why he wrote: "I am already on the point of being sacrificed; the time of my departure has come." He was going to be sacrificed as a victim of hatred against the Lord Jesus, but his death would honor his Lord. He would pay with his life for his faithfulness to Christ. He was ready for it. He was pulling up stakes and folding up his tent, ready to move on.

This does not mean that he was blind to the power of death or the manner in which it was to come. He could speak of death as a sleep from which he would awaken (1 Thess. 4:13 ff.); and he would exclaim: "For me to live is Christ, and to die is gain. . . . My desire is to depart and be with Christ, for that is far better" (Phil. 1:21, 23b).

Despite such confident hope, he knew the meaning of death. He reminded the Christians at Rome: "Sin came into the world through one man, and death through sin, and so death spread to all men because all men sinned" (Rom. 5:12), and in that same letter he called death "the wages of sin" (6:23).

Death is a reminder that we are sinners and that sin pays out fearful wages. In the words of Jesus Himself, death has the power to "destroy both soul and body in hell" (Matt. 10:28).

That ought to make us very humble. We cannot stand beside the casket of anyone and boast of human achievement, because, no matter how great we are in the eyes of others, *when death comes the body is but dust and ashes;* and when the time appointed by God for our death comes, we cannot resist it.

Paul the apostle was aware of this.

Paul L ———————— was aware of this.

They knew what the Bible says about death's power.

Yet they also knew about the word of God which says that Christ has removed the power, the sting of death, so that we can face this enemy unafraid. Because of the promise of God we can repeat the words of the psalmist: "Even though I walk through the valley of the shadow of death, I fear no evil; for Thou art with me" (Ps. 23:4).

II

Such was the confidence of the apostle that he could say: "I have fought the good fight, I have finished the race, I have kept the faith."

It almost sounds like boasting, as though he was saying: "Look what I've done! I have done the best I could, and God is going to have to take me that way."

But anyone who knows the apostle Paul knows full well that he was not talking about merit or earning. In the Gospel he preached he insisted over and over again that our whole relationship to God—the forgiveness of our sins, the approval of the divine Judge, our acceptance into God's family, the gift of eternal life—all this is not a matter of our goodness or merit. It is the free gift of God's grace, given to all who believe in Him, because Jesus died on Calvary's cross to make atonement for our sins. The *only* way to be right with God is to acknowledge our need for His grace and accept it in humble faith.

No, Paul was not talking about earning the favor of God. He was rather talking about *faithfulness.* The treasure that had been given him—the gift of grace, the faith to take hold of that grace, the power to keep holding on to that grace—this, he knew, was the work of the Holy Spirit in his heart. There was no thought of merit in it.

Nevertheless, he could look back on his life with joy that he had been kept in the faith. He had been called to be an apostle. His life was devoted to that cause. He worked hard at it, he sacrificed, he suffered. As a man is happy to see a good harvest after his hard work, so Paul could see the fruits of faith in rich abundance. All of his hard work had been his way of saying "Thank You" to the Lord Jesus for His forgiveness and mercy. He rejoiced to see what had happened in his life—and what was going to happen!

Friends, can we say the same? Are we so committed to our Lord that we can say: "I have fought the good fight . . . I have kept the faith"?

It's sad when an athlete doesn't care, doesn't try; it is sadder still when he loses the prize that might well have been his, if he had just tried.

May God forgive us for our weakness, negligence, forgetfulness!

We lay the life of the departed beside that of the apostle Paul, and we thank God for his faithfulness, so that he could say: "I have kept the faith." Throughout the 52 years of his earthly life he served his Lord well. What confidence that gave him when he faced his departure!

III

Listen to the apostle again: "Henceforth there is laid up for me the crown of righteousness, which the Lord, the righteous Judge, will award to me on that Day."

He was talking about Judgment Day! about the time when he would have to stand before the judgment seat of Christ! For him that was a joyous expectation. He had only one thought in mind—the Lord Jesus was going to give him the crown of life. No maybe, no thought about the possibility of losing it, but a definite expectation.

Because this man knew that all was right with his Lord, the divine Judge had already given His verdict. Paul had stood before the bar of divine justice—Paul, the persecutor, the hater of Christ, the sinner—but he had heard the Judge say: "NOT GUILTY!"—not guilty by reason of the cross of Christ.

You see, friends, what Judgment Day means—whether it is our individual judgment at the time of death, or the universal judgment on the Last Day—what Judgment Day means for the Christian. It will not be a day when we will have to be examined about our life on the basis of how much good or bad there has been. Our sins are not going to be brought into the picture. They have all been sent away in forgiveness, washed away in the blood of Jesus. How often have we not heard the words: "Your sins are forgiven you; go in peace"? Not a single one of those forgiven sins is going to be mentioned. Those who put their trust in Jesus will hear the welcome words: "Come, O blessed of My Father, inherit the kingdom prepared for you from the foundation of the world" (Matt. 25:34). And with that will come the crown of righteousness.

We lay so much stress on this because it is a critical matter. Our whole welfare for this life and the life to come hinges on the cross of Christ. What blessed assurance for those who put their trust in the Lord Jesus! What power for living! What confidence! This faith binds us to the Lord Jesus, and governs and controls our life for His sake.

I am fully aware that there are people who will not accept this. They do not need the Lord Jesus nor want His Gospel. But, friend, if you reject this promise, what have you got in its place? What else is there that can give any assurance, any certainty?

We can be sure! The Lord promises: "Be faithful unto death, and I will give you the crown of life" (Rev. 2:10c).

This is how you should think of your husband, your father, your brother. He has received that crown of life. He has entered all those things prepared for him by his Lord.

He was so "little," so weak and emaciated. But what glory he has now! And there is still more glory to come, when this frail body will be raised to life at the command of our Lord Jesus Christ. That's the Lord's promise, and He has the power to fulfill that promise.

It is often difficult to see the wisdom of the Lord's ways with us, but He has promised to make everything work out for our good. While we are still in this life, He has a purpose for us here. Hold to that purpose. Do not surrender to the influences that would draw you away from Christ, but give your lives to Him in whatever station in life you serve. Let your life be a witness, as this man's was.

Then you can live with confidence and with the eager expectation of seeing your Lord face to face and receiving from Him the crown of life.

Reinhold G. Dohrmann

Related Scripture Readings

2 Kings 2:1-15
John 10:11-15, 27-30
Rom. 8:31-39
Rev. 14:13; 21:1-7; 22:1-5

Suggested Hymns

"I Know that My Redeemer Lives"
"My Course Is Run"
"Beloved, 'It Is Well!' "

FUNERAL (HELPLESS INVALID)

Jesus Loved Him

JOHN 11:35-36

As far as we know, there were but few occasions that caused our Lord and Master to shed tears. Once it was the tragedy that He foresaw for the unbelieving and unrepentant citizens of Jerusalem. Here it was the death of a very dear and close friend.

But who was this friend of Jesus, and what do we know about him?

As we try to answer this question, it may surprise us to realize how meager our information really is. Of course we know his name, Lazarus (whom God helps), and that his home was at Bethany, near Jerusalem. We know that together with his sisters, Martha and Mary, he formed a small family at whose home Jesus stayed on several occasions. We know that he became sick and died and was raised from the dead by Jesus. And that is about all. Not one spoken word of his is recorded. In fact we don't even know whether he was able to speak or not. Not one deed or action of his is recorded, save that he came forth from his tomb at the command of Jesus, and that he was present at the banquet table with Jesus. No mention is made of any work he performed, of any service he rendered, of any help he gave to someone, of any deed of kindness he performed. We read only what others said about him and did for him.

But wait—there is one thing more that we know about Lazarus, and that thing is very meaningful and important. We know that Jesus loved him, warmly and deeply. This fact is mentioned repeatedly by St. John. It was contained in the message the sisters sent to Jesus: "Lord, he whom You love is ill" (11:3). John adds: "Now Jesus loved Martha and her sister *and Lazarus*"(11:5). And he furthermore tells us that the townspeople at Bethany were so impressed that they exclaimed: "See how He loved him!" (11:36).

We know, of course, that the mere silence of Scripture regarding any activity on the part of Lazarus does not absolutely preclude it; and yet, in view of the vivid report of the activity of the sisters, Martha and Mary, their serving, their worship, their sending for Jesus, and their going out to welcome Him, their expressions and actions of faith, I say, this silence regarding any activity on the part of Lazarus is indeed noteworthy. It gives plausibility to the idea of those who think of Lazarus as one in need of the help and service and loving care of others, rather than a strong and self-sufficient person, able to take care of himself and to do these things for other people.

We, therefore, choose to think of Lazarus as representative of that large number of people who, for one reason or another, so deeply need our help and love and compassion; who seemingly exist solely in order to let themselves be helped and cared for and supported and loved for Jesus' sake.

The surpassing beauty of this story lies in the fact that it pictures the deep love of Jesus for Lazarus without even hinting at a single cause or reason on the part of Lazarus to evoke it. It is a picture of the Savior's love, totally unselfish and immaculately pure. But then, is not this the way God's love always is? Undeserving and unworthy as we all are in the sight of the holy and righteous God, He still loves us with a fervent and abiding love.

But just this very fact, that Jesus loved Lazarus so much, raised some searching questions. If Jesus loved him, then why did he become sick, and why did he die? First Martha, and then Mary, raised the question by telling the Master: "Lord, if You hadst been here, my brother would not have died" (11:21). And some of the townspeople expressed their thoughts, saying: "Could not He who opened the eyes of the blind man have kept this man from dying?" (11:37)

Questions like this often arise when we try to reconcile the love of God with pain, and suffering, and infirmity. God's answers are ever full of mystery, but He does show us glimpses of His purposes. To the messengers who brought the sisters' indirect plea for help, He said: "This illness is not unto death; it is for the glory of God, so that the Son of God may be glorified by means of it" (11:4). And to His disciples He said that this was for the strengthening of their faith. Whether it is readily apparent or not, we may rest assured that God's ways and purposes are always good.

If Lazarus indeed was an invalid, his need provided an excellent opportunity to excercise Christian love and compassion. Martha and Mary loved Lazarus and did what they could for him. This was due in part to natural affection, as members of the same family. But their natural love of sisters for a brother was purified and intensified by their faith in and love for God and their Lord Jesus Christ. Any service of love and compassion is hallowed by the teaching of Jesus, that whatever is done to one of the least of His brethren is done to Him.

Some primitive tribes have operated under the rule of getting rid of those who could not work and produce. This heathen spirit has raised its sinister head also among certain "civilized" people, who have espoused the notion that the world would be better off without the many infirm and helpless people. They begrudge them all the care and time and service and money. They are wrong. The world would not be better off without them. The world would be infinitely poorer without the helpless and the needy.

What a cold and heartless place this world would become if there were no need and no opportunity to exercise love and compassion. Since sin has made man naturally selfish and heartless, we have constant need of opportunity and encouragement to exercise the godly virtues of unselfish love and compassion. The opportunity is provided in the persons of special need whom the Lord has placed at our doors or into our homes. The encouragement is given by both the example and the precept of Jesus.

Our departed friend, ——————, was one of those requiring constant care and attention and help. He was never able to work, even at the simplest tasks. He never earned anything, but rather required the support of others. All that he could do was to show, in his own way, his appreciation for the things that were done for him. Was he therefore useless? Not at all. Only they are useless who can work and won't. X . . . was Christ's loved one, made God's child in Holy Baptism, and kept by God's great mercy and power in his baptismal grace. On him his relatives and friends could lavishly expend their own love for Jesus according to the Master's words: "As you did it to one of the least of these My brethren, you did it to Me" (Matt. 25:40). Thus in his own quiet way he served a very useful purpose during his lifetime.

Behold how Jesus loved him! He loved him so much that besides providing for his bodily needs and comforts through his loved ones, He also gave Himself into death for him, so that he might have eternal life in Him. And now the loving Lord Jesus has taken His dear friend out of this troublesome earthly life unto Himself, where perfect joy and well-being and love are in store for him. In the resurrection his frail body will be changed to be like the glorious body of our Lord Jesus (Phil. 3:21). In the mansions above, his infirmities are made whole, and his bliss is unending.

Our great comfort and consolation in this time of sorrow is the knowledge that Jesus loved His friend, and our friend, with such a full and satisfying love that it knows no limits and no end.

The Lord has now concluded the special opportunity of exercising our love for Him through the kind and loving service so generously bestowed upon X . . . That does not, however, mean that there is now no more need for loving care and concern for others. Indeed, in this world there is no lack of opportunity to find someone to serve and love for Jesus' sake. Our Master points us to one such opportunity to show love and compassion when He reminds us: "You always have the poor with you" (Matt. 26:11).

Not only will such unselfish service benefit others, but we ourselves will be blessed by it. It will help our love to grow more pure, more noble, and more rich, while we become more Christlike.

The beautiful demonstration of love so freely given by Jesus to Lazarus, as well as to our departed friend, underscores the unmerited love that is also available to each and every one of us. May we not neglect or spurn it, but in faith firmly grasp the glorious hope therein extended and be with Lazarus and all other believers in the resurrection at the Last Day.

Be still, my soul; the hour is hast'ning on
When we shall be forever with the Lord,
When disappointment, grief, and fear are gone,
Sorrow forgot, love's purest joys restored.
Be still, my soul; when change and tears are past,
All safe and blessed we shall meet at last.

Amen.

Wm. A. Lauterbach

Related Scripture Readings

Luke 7:11-17
John 11:1-15, 21-29
John 14:1-6
1 Cor. 15:53-57
1 Thess. 4:13-18
1 Peter 1:3-9
Rev. 21:1-7

Suggested Hymns

"Blest Be the Tie That Binds"
"Children of the Heavenly Father"
"Asleep in Jesus"
"Love Divine, All Love Excelling"
"Jerusalem the Golden"
"Forever with the Lord"
"Ten Thousand Times Ten Thousand"
"I Know that My Redeemer Lives"
"It Is Not Death to Die"
"I'm But a Stranger Here"

HUMAN RELATIONS (LONELINESS)

I Saw the World's Lonely

MATT. 25:35c, 40; 1 PETER 4:8-11

Whenever I hear the word "stranger," I cannot help but think of someone who is lonely. Of all the words in the English language, perhaps the word "loneliness" provokes the greatest variety of thoughts. We think of a castaway on an island, or a man without a country, or a prisoner in solitary confinement, or a widow or a widower, or a son or daughter away from home, or a crippled young boy standing on the sidelines while others are playing ball.

It is significant to note that each conception of loneliness arising in our minds seems to contain one and the same thought . . . loneliness is never voluntary. It is never a matter of choice or option. On the contrary, loneliness is enforced seclusion. It is found among the young and the old, among the rich and the poor, among the healthy and the sick.

Do you see the world's lonely? Do you see the Lord beckoning you to welcome the stranger into your midst? Christ says: "As you did it to one of the least of these My brethren, you did it to Me"; in that you show your love to the lonely, you show your love to Me.

Do you see those who have become lonely because of the pressures of society? We live in a society that says, "You must get a college education so that you can get a good job so that you can make lots of money, and then you will be happy." As a result, we see many of our young people going away to school. This is, for many of these young people, the first time away from home, away from the shelter of parental care, and away from established friends and familiar surroundings. They find that they are in a sea of unfamiliar objects, unfamiliar people, and unfamiliar textbooks. Many students are strangers—lonely people. Many students will find new friends; will become familiar with their surroundings, and will be able to accept their new responsibilities. Many will overcome their loneliness; but until this happens, what about these students?

In regard to your own children that are away at school, you realize the value of a letter, or a phone call, or a surprise package to boost the morale of one who is lonely. A letter or a phone call is evidence in itself that someone remembers—that someone cares—that someone has included them in their life. This alone can fill a portion of the emptiness of someone's life. Do you see the Lord beckoning you to welcome these students? Greet them, call them, and welcome them as you would do it unto the Lord. Christ says, "Help the lonely. Help these strangers. Do it for Me." And Jesus gives us the power to carry out this task. I am included in God's family through Jesus Christ. God cared so much about me that He gave His only Son for me—Lord, knowing that You care, I can care for these lonely.

It is not only youth who feel the pressures of society. Older people today are finding themselves in an exclusive category. One by one people in a certain age group pass away until one person is standing alone . . . a stranger. Older people are strangers in a society that emphasizes youth and energy. They cannot find jobs because few will hire anyone over 65 years of age, and they too become lonely. Do you see the Lord beckoning you to help the stranger . . . to help the lonely?

Do you see those who have become lonely because of death? Death separates loved ones from one another. How often we have heard the expression from a widow or a widower, "Now I am all alone." The one person who has been with them is gone. The bond of living together is now broken. "We loved one another, we forgave one another, we worked together, we played together, and we worshiped together." All this is now changed to "I live, I work, I play, I worship . . . alone." Do you see the Lord beckoning you to help these people?

Accidental death, compared with so-called natural death, is a greater shock because of the individual's sudden change in status. The housewife may become the breadwinner. The father may also assume the responsibilities that were the mother's. Children must adjust to the loss of a parent. Loneliness sets in. The unfinished tasks keep reminding them of their loss. They are lonely, and because of their new roles in life, they are strangers. Help these people . . . do it for Christ. God forbid that we should think that God has removed His love from us because a loved one has died. Paul in Rom. 8:31-39 writes: "Who shall separate us from the love of Christ?" And he answers the question by saying that not even "tribulation or distress or persecution or famine or nakedness or peril or sword" will do so. Nothing shall separate us from God's love because God has acted for us in Jesus. "In all these things we are more than conquerors through Him who loved us" (v. 37).

Separation, divorces, and broken homes are also contributing factors in making people lonely. Today, more than ever, we see the breaking up of families. Many families are not a close-knit unit, but rather a group of individuals occupying the same house, keeping different schedules, and not doing things together. Members of a family often drift farther and farther apart until separation or divorce occur and the family unit is broken. When this happens, someone is always left alone. Children are pushed from home to home, longing to see their mother or their father. Do you see those who have become lonely? "As you have welcomed the least of these, you have done it to Me."

As Christians we are not alone in this world. We are never strangers. Christ said: "Lo, I am with you always, to the close of the age" (Matt. 28:20).

Do the young students, the older people, the widows, the widowers, and the members of broken homes know this? Do they know that Christ is with them? Tell them what Christ said, but do not stop there. Welcome the stranger. Show the lonely that you care about them. Show them that Christ cares. We are not alone, but included as members of the family of God. Now, we must act to show others that they are no longer strangers and alone. Do it as unto the Lord.

Do you see those who are lonely because they have been avoided? Perhaps the most noticeable acts of avoidance are done in the home. Children are born and not wanted; the place where one lives is a house and not a home; or possibly both parents work and the children must "shift" for themselves. Often, the result is loneliness.

1 John 4:19 (KJV): "We love Him, because He first loved us." Because God first loved us and gave His Son for us, it follows that we love Him. Where there is love for God, there will also be manifestations of that love. The giving of gifts is motivated by the love of the giver for the recipient. How you treat a stranger will reveal the depth of your love for God. "As you are showing your love to the lonely, you are showing it to Me."

The Lord says, "Above all hold unfailing your love for one another" (1 Peter 4:8). "Above all, hold unfailing your love for one another." Never fail to show your love! What a profound thought! Lord, help us to show our love to those whom we have avoided.

Why should we show our love? Because "love covers a multitude of sins." True love forgives every sin and transgression and reaches out to help and to serve.

Do you see those who have been avoided in that they were not shown hospitality? Hospitality seems to be a forgotten art. We could say that love for our Savior is our motive for action and that hospitality is the action. It is an action that proceeds from a heart motivated by love toward someone else. Hospitality is greeting the stranger in church, welcoming the lonely into your home for fellowship, sharing the Word of God, sharing your material blessings, and doing all without grumbling or complaining or bragging. The Lord is asking you to show your hospitality to those who are strangers and are lonely.

Do you see those who have been avoided in that people have not used their gifts for others? Many people would not be lonely if they knew about Christ, if they knew that Christ was with them or if they knew that someone was interested in them. We could be making people lonely by not using our gifts for others, by not showing that we care—truly care for others. Peter says that we should employ or use these gifts for one another, "as good stewards of God's varied grace" (1 Peter 4:10). God has given us our gifts; He has entrusted these gifts to our care. We are to use them for His purposes. We are only stewards. God is still the Owner. Our duties as stewards have not been discharged when we have set aside 5, 10, or 20 percent for church and charity. Being good stewards means that we faithfully and gratefully use all the blessings God has given us, even though we may already have supported His work with liberal gifts.

We are to be loving, hospitable, employing our gifts as good stewards in order that God may be glorified. Act in answer to the Lord's beckoning and with the power He supplies. Be Christians 24 hours a day. May all of us, under the guidance of the Holy Spirit, be able to say in the future, "We saw the world's lonely; we saw them and we welcomed them." "God so loved the world that He gave His only Son. . . ." God, move us to so love the lonely that we might give our lives to them as unto You.

Donald L. Johnson

Related Scripture Readings

Matt. 25:31-46
Rom. 8:31-39
1 Corinthians 13
Phil. 2:1-11
James 2:14-17

Suggested Hymns

"Come, Ye Disconsolate"
"Abide with Me!"
"O Blessed Holy Trinity"
"I'm But a Stranger Here"
"Blest Be the Tie that Binds"
"Drawn to the Cross"
"Now Thank We All Our God"

INDEPENDENCE DAY

Compassion, the Fiber of Freedom

LUKE 14:12-14

The Fourth of July, Independence Day, suggests many themes, but none quite as stirring as freedom. America's national history resounds with the heroic stories, the mystique, and some myths of our founding fathers in behalf of freedom. But freedom is an elusive word, with different meanings for different people. Jefferson, architect of the Declaration of Independence, kept household slaves. One man's freedom often meant another man's bondage. Freedom became license. In abhorrence over such abuse Luther spoke out in an especially vivid way at the time of the civil uprisings in Wittenberg, 1522, stating: "When you have suckled long enough, do not cut off the breast, but let your brother be suckled also."

This reminds us that there is another ingredient in our freedom, essential to its maintenance and survival. It may be described by phrases like "with liberty *and* justice for all"; or by the Four freedoms enunciated by President Franklin Roosevelt in 1941—freedom of speech and religion, and freedom from want and fear; or by the famous words of Lincoln in his Second Inaugural Address, when the nation was bowed down with horrible civil war, "with malice toward none, with charity for all." Then there's the inscription on the pedestal of the Statue of Liberty in New York harbor, the moving words of Emma Lazarus: "Give me your tired, your poor, your huddled masses yearning to breathe free. . . . Send these, the homeless, tempest-tossed to me."

Obviously, there is more that holds freedom together than the right to do as one pleases. A good number of our forefathers came to these shores seeking freedom from want and oppression not only for themselves but also for their neighbors. The history of our land, this "home of the brave," contained a good amount of altruistic spirit and was written in such terms as "the haven of the homeless and tempest-tossed." James Madison, writing in the *National Gazette,* Dec. 20, 1792, posed the question: "Who are the best keepers of the people's liberties?" His answer: "The people themselves. The sacred trust can be nowhere so safe as in the hands most interested in preserving it. What a perversion of the natural order of things to make *power* the primary and central object of the social system, and liberty but its satellite." Madison was among the forefathers who put a high premium on the value of religious faith for our country, if liberty was to prevail. Since then it has often been observed, and history has borne witness, that Christianity can well enough survive without democracy; but it must be seriously doubted that a democracy like ours could long survive without Christianity.

The glue that holds the nation together and preserves liberty, so that this noble experiment of government by the people, of the people, and for the people does not immediately go apart or perish, is *compassion.* This is the key element. It seasons liberty and provides the ingredient that can turn it to good. Our text portrays it as the fruit of faith in a graphic way. Christ elicits it from His followers, also from us in this land of the free. The unique contribution of Christian faith is right at this point, blazoned on liberty's tapestry. It is

Compassion, the Fiber of Freedom

The heathen world, especially Roman and Greek culture, often looked upon compassion as a sign of weakness. Christians, too, have at times characterized it as a counsel for the perfect only. St. Augustine, as a matter of fact, held the opinion that "a ruler should not humble himself too much, lest government come to be despised." Luther read this and commented: "This is purely secular, heathen advice, not Christian, and I wish he had left it out, because it smells, like Adam's barrel or hogshead; but one can forgive a person like Augustine, since even the godly are not perfect."

The fact is, as Luther points out, that in these words of our text Jesus is talking to you and me about compassion. He spoke these words in the home of a leading Pharisee who had invited Him and special guests for dinner. Christ gave all of them an object lesson they would never forget. He healed a man sick with dropsy, even though it was the sabbath, when nothing was to interfere with the prescribed ceremonial way of doing things. And then Jesus told a parable about humility, when He noticed how the guests scrambled for the choice seats at the dinner. Rather take a lower seat, Jesus said, and if it is the host's pleasure, he will direct you to one of the so-called upper, choicer seats.

Then follow the words of our text concerning compassion, when Jesus noticed that the dinner guests consisted only of the man's friends, brethren, kinsmen, and rich neighbors. Undoubtedly what He said, as He pointed out this fact, was not meant primarily as rebuke; nor was it intended to embarrass the host before his guests; nor did Jesus in a patronizing spirit wish to humiliate people and vaunt Himself over them. It was merely to drive home the point, as Luther puts it, that they who are religious, or godly, or really and truly pious, are ready to "put it," that is, their Christianity or Christian walk of life, "on the scales and weigh it according to God's Word." Only genuine compassion could balance it out!

Christ's own life and ministry were the very epitome of such compassion. When He saw the multitude, Christ saw them

—as sheep that were scattered, needing a shepherd (Matt. 9:36-38);
—as hungry, needing bread, especially the Bread of Life (Matt. 15:32);
—as sick, needing healing, in body and soul (Matt. 14:14);
—as fearful, under the shroud of death, as the widow of Nain, whose son lay dead; as Jairus, whose little daughter had succumbed; or as Mary and Martha, who had lost their beloved brother Lazarus—all of them needing to know Him who was the Resurrection and the Life.

And when they came in faith, Christ never refused them either bodily or spiritual help, most often responding to their needs even before they asked. Moreover, nothing ever took precedence over His mission of mercy, as now on the sabbath He healed the man sick of dropsy before their amazed eyes, doing it with such authority and evident Lordship, showing that the sabbath, as all other things, belonged to Him and that the sabbath and the other laws which they kept so fanatically were now at an end, since He, the Messiah, was now Himself present on earth, in their midst.

Anguish filled His holy, compassionate heart for sinful mankind

—for the respectable classes so-called;
—for the despised among men, the publicans and sinners;

—for the whole sick body of mankind in general.

He could "sympathize with our weaknesses" (Heb. 4:15 KJV). Above all—and forever the most incredibly mysterious wonder of God's love for sinful mankind, which we will never be able to understand, nor fully appreciate—He brought the ultimate sacrifice for our sin and for the sins of all the world.

Isaiah, already 700 years earlier, foretold by divine inspiration how the Messiah, the Suffering Servant,

—bore our griefs;
—carried our sorrows;
—was wounded for our transgressions;
—was bruised for our iniquities;
—had the iniquity of us all laid on Him (Isaiah 53).

In the New Testament, Christ's atoning sacrifice on Calvary's cross was the center of the apostle Paul's preaching: "Christ, who knew no sin was made to be sin for us!" "For our sake He [God] made Him [Christ] to be sin who knew no sin" (2 Cor. 5:21). As for Paul, so also for John (and the rest of the disciples), the same truth formed the heart and core of his message: "Hereby perceive we the love of God, because He laid down His life for us" (1 John 3:16 KJV).

Compassion, wondrous, inexplicable compassion, is the one word that characterized our Savior's whole mission and ministry for people on earth. By it Christ in very fact set us free, with the most incredible freedom we will ever know and have, righteous and holy before God in heaven, through faith in our blessed Redeemer's sacrifice!

Now, as Jesus dealt in greatest compassion with us, so we are exhorted to compassion for those with whom we have to do. We ought to be filled with compassion for one another, as the apostle Peter later wrote. Peter himself had tasted deeply of Christ's love. Hence he spoke with authority and from rich experience when he stated: "It is God's will that by doing right you should put to silence the ignorance of foolish men. Live as free men, yet without using your freedom as a pretext for evil; but live as servants of God" (1 Peter 2:15-16).

The apostle Peter spoke these words in the context of his appeal to Christians to be responsible, obedient citizens, whatever the form of government. Neither his nor first of all Christ's appeal to compassion was a counsel merely of perfection, or for the so-called perfect, as was sometimes taught within Christendom, but the perfectly proper counsel for every follower of the Lord. Compassion is not a Christian luxury, which some have and others not, but a Christian necessity! Jesus makes this very plain. In our text He spells it out in unmistakable terms. It is to be there for all the needy around us, whatever their necessity. The same truth is the main emphasis in the parable of the wicked servant, when the Lord of the servant asks, "Should not you have had mercy on your fellow servant, as I had mercy on you?" (Matt. 18:23-35)

So, Jesus is not first of all lecturing us about the kind of guests we should or should not invite into our homes, though He is touching a few sensitive spots nonetheless as regards our attitude toward the people around us. Principally He is lecturing us about the unfeeling sort of insensitivity over against our neighbor, whatever his class, color, or station, which can pass a man by, like the priest and the Levite in the story of the good Samaritan. It's the kind of insensitivity that considers outward observance of the sabbath, or religious rules, more important than human need.

Luther preached an extremely beautiful sermon on our text in 1544, at Torgau, for the dedication of the first newly built church since the Reformation had begun in 1517. Among other things Luther noted that

—there are God-given stations in life,
—but that God honors them all;
—that heaven is not for the high and mighty only,
—but that the poorest also have the riches of God;
—and that pride affects both prince and peasant alike.

When it comes to dealing with mankind around us, Luther pointed out, the principle that obtains is that "need breaks all laws," all barriers, customs, and ways of doing things. When the Reformer explained the Fifth Commandment in his notable Good Works treatise of 1520, he emphasized that the key word in understanding this commandment is meekness, *Sanftmuetigkeit,* softheartedness, that is, soft- or tenderheartedness in the sense of a gentle spirit. This is not the kind of meekness which bows condescendingly before those who in turn can do us good; that would be a false, counterfeit kind. True meekness, Luther states, is the spirit of tenderheartedness towards those who cannot return the favor to us, or who won't do us good in return, but who in fact may return evil for good. To curb one's heart in such instances,

—to think kindly of others,
—to wish well and the best for men of such stripe,
—to care for those who could not care less,
—to pray for those who may bite the hand that feeds them,
—to speak well of them,
—to do them good,

that is the real test of Christian compassion! And Luther's point is very clear: If that is what God wants, and if God will be paid in no other coin, of what use is it for us to run around performing great works which are not commanded and neglect those that are? "Love and need take precedence over all laws. There is no law which ought not bend or give way to love, even if an angel from heaven made it! So God is teaching us how we ought to humble ourselves before others," Luther states. The message is plain: compassion is the hallmark of Christian living in the midst of a troubled world, in dealing with the sick, sinful body of humankind.

Compassion is also the glue that holds liberty or freedom together in a land like ours. It keeps freedom from becoming license, from going sour and becoming ruthless anarchy and heartless self-serving. The Christian dare never forget "the little ones" of whom Jesus speaks, the forgotten ones of society. This includes those who revile and persecute you, Jesus reminds us in the Beatitudes. When Tetzel, Luther's bitter opponent in the indulgence squabble, who called for the Reformer's neck because he opposed the papal sale, lay dying and cast off by his erstwhile friends and supporters, it was Luther who came to his aid and wrote a tender, compassionate letter of forgiveness, interceding for him as for a friend.

A believer knows that his sanctification of life, of which compassion is a main ingredient, is God's will for him; that it is God's good pleasure; and that in His grace God rewards it and will bring rich recompense at the resurrection of the just. This does not change the great central truth of our salvation, that Christ was delivered for our sins, nailed to Calvary's tree, and raised again for our justification. But it does underscore Jesus' very solemn promise: "As you did it to one of the least of these My brethren, you did it to Me" (Matt. 25:40). This is a precious truth, with a precious pledge.

The freedom we as Christians enjoy is never seen in any other light. Liberty, as the Christian sees it, is sewn tightly together with the fibers of compassion. This fruit of faith is our heavenly Father's gracious goodwill.

Eugene F. Klug

Related Scripture Readings

Mark 2:23-3:6
John 8:12-59
Rom. 13:1-10
Gal. 5:1-14
1 Peter 2:11-25

Suggested Hymns

"All People that on Earth Do Dwell"
"O God of Mercy, God of Might"
"Jesus, the Very Thought of Thee"
"Before the Lord We Bow"
"God Bless Our Native Land"
"All Ye That on the Earth Do Dwell"
"Guide Me, O Thou Great Jehovah"
"Lord of Glory, Who Hast Bought Us"

LABOR DAY

Conclusions of a 5:00 Commuter

ECCL. 2:18-25; EPH. 2:8-10

Labor Day was originally set aside in order to recognize working people. When we think of laborers from the past, we have images of sweatshops, child labor, and many of the inequities present during the industrialization of America. The struggle of workers to unite in order to present a common front to employers and to gain justice in the working place is also part of our imagery on Labor Day. Much has been accomplished over the years, including job safety, higher wages, labor laws, and pension plans.

Today we do not celebrate Labor Day very well. For most people it merely represents the final weekend of the summer.

Perhaps this is because the whole nature of work and of labor has changed. The image of the laborer has been that of someone who worked with his hands at skilled and unskilled vocations. In the book *Great Expectations: America and the Baby Boom Generation,* by Langdon Y. Jones (Coward, McCann and Geoghegan, 1980), this observation about labor in America is made: "After World War II, though, America began a historic changeover from a manufacturing economy to a service economy. Between 1950 and 1974, only one million out of the twenty-seven million new jobs created were in goods-related industries like steel, agriculture, mining, and construction . . ." (page 167). Labor has definitely changed. In addition, we can no longer speak in terms of working *men,* for vast numbers of women have entered the labor force and have crashed through the barriers of once male-dominated jobs. Jones observes: "In the end, what the country has seen was a twenty-five-year surge in which the American working force was remade by women. Of the 43 million women now working—more than half of the adult female population—some nine million of them . . . joined in the 1970s" (page 173).

In a manner of speaking, then, there is hardly anyone who does not fall into the category of being a laborer. At least 8 hours per day, 5 days per week, 50 weeks per year, and 40 years of one's life are involved in labor. That means 2,000 weeks and 80,000 hours of life are spent in one's daily occupation. "What do you do?" someone asks of us. When we provide the answer to that question, a certain value, social class, and economic status have already been assigned to us. Work is important.

Today, then, we are going to talk about work, where we spend almost one-third of our adult life; work, which stamps us as to "who we are"; work, which produces the earning power that enhances life or can destroy it; work, which can be meaningless frustration or extremely fulfilling; work, where time hangs heavy or is filled with meaning; work, something we yearn for when we don't have it and can despise when we do have it.

We look at work through the eyes of the writer of Ecclesiastes, a man filled with much pessimism, but a man who perhaps gets at the mood of Christian people who spend so much time at work, yet wonder what it's really all about. We shall also look at work through the eyes and the words of the apostle St. Paul and begin to learn how our work fits into God's plan.

I. Conclusion No. 1: Labor by Itself Is Meaningless

The writer of Ecclesiastes begins by saying: "I hated all my toil in which I had toiled under the sun, seeing that I must leave it to the man who will come after me. . . . What has a man from all the toil and strain with which he toils beneath the sun? For all his days are full of pain, and his work is a vexation; even in the night his mind does not rest. This also is vanity."

One might call this the lament of the 5:00 commuter. Today's commuter might say it differently. As he drives home from work he might reflect: "What's the use? What's the use? Nothing works out right. What's the use? Seventeen years with the same firm, learning all there is to learn, climbing up from position to position, and for what? Younger men, ambitious and smart, beginning to see how tired I am, knowing I'm beginning to stumble, wait to push me out. Even if I survive, so what? Who gets what I've built up? My son couldn't care less. No, he cares, he cares enough to reject not only what I've done but what I've become. What's the use? My hands shake, my stomach always aches, I can't sleep at night, and each morning I have to drag myself out of bed to face another day. I live for the weekends, but in order to keep even, most of my weekend is spent with work from the office, and the rest of the time is spent in worrying. I have no energy left over to love my wife or to get reacquainted with my children. We're a family of polite and sometimes not-so-polite strangers. What's the use? What's the purpose of it all? What's the use?"

Whether it is the farmer coming in from the field, the housewife looking at a pile of laundry ("Do they really think this reappears in their drawers and closets by magic?"), the assembly line worker, or the executive, this represents the universal question. It is a good question: "What's it all about?"

The writer of Ecclesiastes came to the tentative conclusion that one's work doesn't have much purpose. He wonders further if this is the way he wants to spend his life.

Is that the purpose of our work—to earn a living, to provide for our needs, and to enhance our life? The Christian commuter realizes that there is something selfish and shortsighted about that. He wonders to himself about how much he really needs. He wonders if his luxuries have become necessities. He wonders if he is buying happiness with his job. If he is buying happiness, then why isn't he happier? He realizes that whatever successes he has will die with him. Perhaps he remembers the rich fool in Jesus' parable who found out too late that work as a goal in itself is a false goal. The rich fool worked for the "when" time. It has always been that way: when! The rich fool died with the echo that the 5:00 commuter perhaps also hears: "Fool!"

The Old Testament writer lamented that "sometimes a man who has toiled with wisdom and knowledge and skill must leave all to be enjoyed by a man who did not toil for it." The contemporary 5:00 commuter would perhaps say it differently: "What can a father leave his son or daughter in material wealth? The farm, the business, perhaps. Intellect? Ph.D.? The vice-presidency? And will they accept that life-style and all that it connotes, from a father who died too early and unhappily of a coronary from overwork?"

That's Conclusion No. 1 from our commuter. What he has been working for is useless. He has had the wrong goals. Perhaps the worker several centuries before Christ could go home from his fields, gather his wife and children around him, and share this knowledge with them. Perhaps they would politely listen, and then do what they wanted anyway. But will the 20th-century commuter have that chance? His children won't stop long enough to listen, for in an age of change and youth orientation, what can the old say to the young? And his wife, having had a rough day and worrying about her husband's excess weight, smoking, and drinking, would only get more upset by his sudden despondency.

II. Conclusion No. 2: Enjoy Labor Under God the Creator

"There is nothing better for a man than that he should eat and drink, and find enjoyment in his toil. This also, I saw, is from the hand of God; for apart from Him who can eat or who can have enjoyment?" This is the tentative conclusion that the writer of Ecclesiastes comes to in our text.

The mood of the 5:00 commuter changes. He is not exactly leaping for joy, but he does have a more solemn certainty about his work and his life. If success does not last, he thinks to himself, and if living for the "when" time is an empty goal, then what does last, and what is a proper goal? God lasts, he thinks. He remembers Jesus' Sermon on the Mount. He recalls the image of the lilies of the field and the birds of the air. "Don't worry!" Jesus had said. "Your heavenly Father knows your needs. Seek the Kingdom first, and everything else will follow." I must relax, he thinks to himself, and enjoy, and trust.

These insights begin to open his eyes to daily life. Work is not an evil thing. Work can be very good. It is part of God's creation. Even in Eden our first parent was given the "labor" of naming the animals. Adam had been working for God and cooperating with God. The farmer surely must see this cooperation as he plows the fields and watches the plants burst forth from the soil and then gathers in the harvest. The laborer too can see this in the finished product and in the person who will use the product. Yet this is hard to see today. In the days when labor and the finished product were not so far removed from each other, perhaps it was possible. In those days the worker could sign his work. Johann Sebastian Bach could begin and end his compositions with words of praise toward the Lord. A worker laboring on a piece of furniture could finish not only what could be seen but also what was not seen simply because he had pride in his workmanship. Today, in a throwaway age, in a mass-produced culture, in a service-oriented economy, it is hard to do. We are often far removed from the end product or the person who will use that product.

Yet this may not represent an impossible dilemma but rather an opportunity to have a greater and deeper vision of God and His presence in our daily lives. How real is God for us? The apostle Paul saw Him everywhere when he wrote: "Whether you eat or drink, or whatever you do, do all to the glory of God" (1 Cor. 10:31). Theologian Dr. Martin Marty wrote a book that was titled *The Hidden Discipline.* It had to do with seeing beyond what our eyes see and obeying and serving and praising God far beyond what is apparent on the surface. It is to look into things with the mind of God. It is to realize that God is working in and through us, whether we are working with a word processor, a farm combine, or a wrench. To earn a living, to enjoy life each day, to see the benefit of our labor is not wrong. There is one thing about the lilies and the birds: They not only don't worry; they don't feel guilty about their work.

As the 5:00 commuter nears his home, the conclusions he has arrived at will pull him through this day, and maybe he will sleep tonight. Yet this is not enough to take him much farther than that, for his conclusions are too much like a lesson in positive thinking with God thrown in for good measure. These are good preparatory thoughts, but they are not the kinds of insights that change lives and make them whole. The insights he needs are evident especially in the words of our text from St. Paul: "For by grace you have been saved through faith; and this is not your own doing, it is the gift of God—not because of works, lest any man should boast. For we are His workmanship, created in Christ Jesus for good works, which God prepared beforehand, that we should walk in them" (Eph. 2:8-10).

III. Conclusion No. 3: Our Labor Has Been Transformed into Praise

If we are to understand our labor and are to place it into the context of a life that is truly whole, we need to shift our focus from Labor Day to the Day of the Cross. On the Day of the Cross we who labor—whether farmer, merchant, housewife, or whatever—must come with *no* job, *no* status, *nothing* except: "We brought nothing into the world . . ." (1 Tim. 6:7). The Day of the Cross is the day of God's labor, not ours. It is the day of grace.

It is Good Friday: "For by grace you have been saved through faith; and this is not your own doing, it is the gift of God." The Day of the Cross is the day of our death with Jesus Christ.

It is also our day of resurrection: "For we are His workmanship, created in Christ Jesus for good works, which God prepared beforehand, that we should walk in them." The Master Worker has produced a new creation, His beautiful workmanship fashioned through Jesus Christ: Me! I am not a mass-produced product, but a singular creation brought to life by the blood of Jesus Christ and the working of the Holy Spirit. I am not a nameless and bland object labeled with the brand name of "Christian," but a new person named by God and carrying His name from Holy Baptism onward. I am not a throwaway person with a shelf life of 70-plus years, but a precious child of God whose life will last forever.

Our vocation is a reflection of who and whose we are through Jesus Christ. Our daily work is God's work in us, "for we are His workmanship, created . . . for good works." Our daily work is not an end in itself. That is far too limited and limiting of our personhood. Rather, our daily work is part of our walk with God. It is part of the means toward the highest goal and end of life—to pray, praise, and give thanks to God.

Nowhere does Scripture indicate that one task is higher than another. When Scripture speaks of higher work—for instance, in the work of the ordained minister—it does so only in terms of greater opportunities to *serve.* Rather, the Bible always speaks in terms of seeing *God* as the end result of labor. That truth elevates whatever our work is, no matter how menial, into praise of God. That truth also removes pride from whatever task elevates us in the eyes of the world and shows us the goal of our high place—the praise of God. That truth also reminds us that our talents and abilities and knowledge are all gifts from God, to whom we are privileged to offer praise through our labors 8 hours each day, 5 days each week, 50 weeks each year.

Conclusion

The 5:00 commuter drives his car into the garage and walks into the kitchen with a bounce to his step. He has learned something this late summer afternoon. He has learned that success alone is an empty god. He has learned that he can enjoy life, for *God* is the Giver. What places God at the center and life into God's giving hand is the gift of God Himself in His self-giving love in Christ. Now in relieved thanksgiving our commuter calls his wife and children to him to share his insights and his joy. Will they listen? Will they see? Will they join him in thanksgiving? That part of the story we deliver into your hands. For we are the commuters to whom God addresses this word.

Richard G. Kapfer

Related Scripture Readings

Gen. 2:15	Eccl. 9:10	1 Cor. 15:58
Gen. 3:19	Hag. 2:4	2 Thess. 3:10-13

Suggested Hymns

"Forgive Us, Lord, for Shallow Thankfulness"
"Lord, Lead the Way the Savior Went"
"With the Lord Begin Thy Task"
"Now the Shades of Night Are Gone"
"The Radiant Sun Shines in the Skies"
"Awake, My Soul, and with the Sun"
"Take My Life that It May Be"
"Oh, that the Lord Would Guide My Ways"

MEMORIAL DAY

Greater Love . . .

JOHN 15:11-13

"Greater love has no man than this, that a man lay down his life for his friends." These words of our Lord come right after His command that we love one another. Such self-sacrifice is remembered in our observances of Memorial Day. This national custom to commemorate those whom we respect and honor started after the Civil War as a tribute to the casualties and as a symbol of national reconciliation. Today Memorial Day services have been broadened to remember all who are no longer living, including loved ones from our family, members from our congregation, dear friends and relatives, and countless others now in eternal peace and rest with our Lord Jesus Christ.

At the gates of Arlington National Cemetery on a recent Memorial Day hundreds of flower-bearing survivors stood in line to ask officials for grave numbers of their loved ones. Ten to fifteen service personnel are still buried daily at Arlington Cemetery, which holds the remains of about 185,000 veterans and members of their families. Thousands of visitors watched the Vice President lay a wreath at the Tomb of the Unknown Soldier, with its inscription: "Here Rests in Honored Glory an American Soldier Known but to God." During the previous year millions of tourists had visited this tomb, watched day and night by a special honor guard. At the cemetery's Old Amphitheater former hostages of Iran and families of military personnel missing in action paid tribute to the eight servicemen who died in the aborted raid to rescue the hostages. Relatives of the dead men accepted medals from former hostages who attended the ceremony. It was sponsored by "No Greater Love," a 10-year-old family organization to honor servicemen. The former charge d'affairs at the embassy in Tehran told the large group: "God bless the memory of these men. God bless their families."

Our Lord has reminded us that the greatest love a person can have for his friends is to give his life for them. How can we forget? On Memorial Day many are remembered for personal sacrifices made for country, for freedom, for loved ones, and even for you and me. Christ simply said "for his friends."

It is proper, then, that we should remember at this time the many who out of love and loyalty sacrificed so much for our country. One can recall the experiences of the men who had signed the Declaration of Independence, who acted not only for themselves or for the 3 million inhabitants of the 13 colonies, but were ready to pledge their lives to secure God-given freedoms for generations unborn. For this cause they were willing to endure amazing trials and hardships. Five of the 56 signers were captured by the British and then condemned as traitors. It was reported that they were tortured before dying. Twelve signers of the Declaration had their homes ransacked and destroyed. Nine died from wounds or hardships of the Revolutionary War. Two lost sons who had enlisted in the Revolutionary Army; another had two sons who were made prisoners of war. When the word was spread that the Declaration had been signed, General George Washington was in command of the Continental Army encamped near New York. He was threatened with defeat when he wrote this prayerful petition: "Almighty God, we make our earnest prayer that Thou wilt keep the United States in Thy holy protection; that Thou wilt incline the hearts of the citizens to . . . entertain a brotherly love and affection for one another. . . . Grant our supplication, we beseech Thee, through Jesus Christ our Lord. Amen."

We thank God that we live in a country where our freedoms have been well established and protected. In the world today millions of men, women, and children suffer every form of social injustice, oppression, religious persecution, and political tyranny. We thank God for life in a land where such individual freedoms have not been threatened or forgotten. Especially as Christians we are mindful of the blessing in our freedom of worship. We have the freedom to profess our own personal faith; to worship our God, how, where, and when we wish; and to receive religious instruction without fear or restriction from the state or government. Many have suffered much so that these freedoms could be preserved in our nation today; we do not forget them.

Today we do not forget the men and women in the Armed Forces who have been ready to serve and defend our country. Some have even suffered and died for us. And they are well known to us, because many from our midst have worn the military uniform and served our nation in war and peace in all parts of the world. You may think immediately of your parents, or brother or sister, son or daughter, relative or friend. Today over 8,000 servicemen and -women, members of our church, are serving in the armed forces. And our church body has not forgotten them. Your Armed Forces Commission every month still provides a Ministry-by-Mail to these thousands of service personnel and to members of their families. Spiritually speaking they have been well prepared. They too can be ready to declare with Paul: "I have fought the good fight, I have finished the race, I have kept the faith. Henceforth there is laid up for me the crown of righteousness, which the Lord, the righteous judge, will award to me on that Day, and not only to me but also to all who have loved His appearing" (2 Timothy 4:7-8).

There have been many accounts of the unselfish devotion of chaplains in the service. One story will never be forgotten. During World War II in the icy North Atlantic off Greenland four chaplains of different faiths made a sacrifice that stirred our nation. It was shortly after 1:00 a.m. on a stormy February night; the *USS Dorchester* with 900 men was sailing to Greenland. A torpedo exploded in the engine room, knocking out all communications and tearing a gaping hole in the hull. Later it was told how frightened men groped their way out of the dark holds, some losing their life jackets in the panic and confusion of the sinking ship. The four chaplains were heard comforting the terrified, helping corpsmen treat the wounded, and then assisting others to leave the ship to reach the limited space of the overcrowded life rafts in the water. Many could not hope to live more than 40 minutes in the freezing sea. When a frightened young soldier cried that he had lost his life jacket and that he couldn't swim, one of the chaplains said, "Take this. I'm staying. I won't need it." None of the survivors could remember which chaplain made the first offer. But then almost immediately all four chaplains had given away their life jackets and voiced their determination to remain with the ship. With arms linked, they stood on the slanting deck of the sinking ship while urging men to board the last overcrowded raft. When last seen and heard they were praying: "Our Father who art in heaven, hallowed be Thy name; Thy kingdom come; Thy will be done on earth as it is in heaven. . . ."

And we are mindful of our own pastors for the military, chaplains who have volunteered their services to minister to military personnel under peaceful or battle conditions in all parts of the world. Personal sacrifice, separation from families, danger, and even death itself have not deterred chaplains of our church from their mission to serve men, women, and their families in the military.

A distinctive marble memorial for chaplains of our church was erected and dedicated in the main entrance hall of Concordia Historical Institute, St. Louis, on St. Martin of Tours Day, Nov. 11, 1981. The sculpture of this memorial depicts Martin of Tours dividing his military cape with his sword to share it with a ragged and cold beggar at the city gate of Amiens. From this act of charity and mercy eventually were derived the words "chaplain" and "chapel" in our language today. For Lutheran chaplains there is a special historic relationship to St. Martin of Tours Day, because 500 years ago the day-old Martin Luther was baptized and named after this famous Christian leader from the fourth century A.D.

In a large book on the white marble stand before this chaplains' memorial are the names of over 600 chaplains of our church who ministered to the military since 1862. Our first chaplain was the Lutheran pastor Friedrich W. Richmann, who served as chaplain for the 58th Regiment of Ohio Volunteers during the Civil War. And much could be told about the experiences and ministries of other Lutheran chaplains to service personnel and their families. We know that they were ready and present to strengthen and counsel many stationed for the first time far from home and loved ones. They were there to comfort and reassure the sick and the wounded and the dying—sometimes at the cost of being themselves injured or killed during the very act of ministering to others. With pastoral subtleness Paul had reminded the church in Rome that such pastors are needed: "But how are men to call upon Him in whom they have not believed? And how are they to believe in Him of whom they have never heard? And how are they to hear without a preacher? And how can men preach unless they are sent? As it is written, 'How beautiful are the feet of those who preach good news!' " (Rom. 10:14-15). So we too can remember our chaplains, who were not hesitant to answer this oft-times urgent call for service to God and country.

However, in every Christian memorial service must be remembered the sacrificial love of our God: "For God so loved the world that He gave His only Son, that whoever believes in Him should not perish but have eternal life" (John 3:16). We know that our Lord was ready to lay down His life for us. While Christ was with His disciples on earth, He would again and again alert them about the certainty of His own crucifixion and death.

Even before returning to Jerusalem for the last time, Jesus had clearly voiced to His own disciples His readiness to lay down His life for us. While in the district of Caesarea Philippi with Jesus and His disciples, Simon Peter had made his confession: "You are the Christ, the Son of the living God," and "from that time Jesus began to show His disciples that He must go to Jerusalem and suffer many things from the elders and chief priests and scribes, and be killed, and on the third day be raised." Peter had been quick to criticize such intentions: "God forbid, Lord! This shall never happen to You." Remember our Lord's response to Peter? "Get behind Me, Satan! You are a hindrance to Me; for you are not on the side of God, but of men" (Matt. 16:13-23). Such a sacrificial act of love was no surprise because it had been predicted many years before by the prophet Isaiah: "Surely He has borne our griefs and carried our sorrows; yet we esteemed Him stricken, smitten by God, and afflicted. But He was wounded for our transgressions, He was bruised for our iniquities; upon Him was the chastisement that made us whole, and with His stripes we are healed" (Is. 53:4-5).

Don't we regularly remember the sacrifical love of our Lord whenever we partake of the Lord's Supper? It also becomes a memorial service, as Paul reminded the church in Corinth: "For I received from the Lord what I also delivered to you, that the Lord Jesus on the night when He was betrayed took bread, and when He had given thanks, He broke it, and said, 'This is My body which is for you. *Do this in remembrance of Me.* In the same way also the cup, after supper, saying, 'This cup is the new covenant in My blood. *Do this, as often as you drink it, in remembrance of me. For as often as you eat this bread and drink this cup, you proclaim the Lord's death until He comes"*(1 Cor. 11:23-26). What greater significance can any memorial service have for you and me?

Finally, the overtone of any Christian memorial service is a victorious one. "Who shall separate us from the love of Christ? Shall tribulation, or distress, or persecution, or famine, or nakedness, or peril, or sword? . . . No, in all these things we are more than conquerors through Him who loved us. For I am sure that neither death, nor life, nor angels, nor principalities, nor things present, nor things to come, nor powers, nor height, nor depth, nor anything else in all creation, will be able to separate us from the love of God in Christ Jesus our Lord" (Rom. 8:35-39). Amen.

M. S. Ernstmeyer

Related Scripture Readings

Ps. 23:4	John 10:11	1 Tim. 2:1	2 Tim. 4:6-8
Luke 15:3-7	John 10:27-29	1 Tim. 6:12	Rev. 21:4
Luke 19:17	John 14:1-3		

Suggested Hymns

"Onward, Christian Soldiers"
"The Strife Is O'er, the Battle Done"
"Be Still, My Soul"
"Jesus, Savior, Pilot Me"
"All Who Would Valiant Be"
"Who Trusts in God, a Strong Abode"
"A Mighty Fortress Is Our God"
"Stand Up!—Stand Up for Jesus"

MOTHER'S DAY

What Mothers Can Do

2 TIM. 1:5

Mothers, how would you like to be remembered after you're gone? as a good cook? neat housekeeper? a friend and confidant? a nice hostess? one who mended socks and patched jeans? one who taught your children to be hard workers? taught them responsibility? All of these would be fine, but this one would be the best: "My mother? She's the one who led me to Jesus."

There are times when we feel insignificant, of no account, not very important or crucial in the scheme of things. Maybe a lady who lived long ago felt that way. She had her elderly mother living with them; she had one son and had the normal problems bringing him up; her husband was not even a believer, although he was good to them. All she accomplished was that she shared her faith in Christ with her son, who used to love to talk with her and his grandmother about God and prayer and heaven. . . . By now you've guessed who we're talking about. Her name was Eunice, and her son, who became rather famous, was Timothy.

What can a mother do? Lots of good and worthwhile activities, but above them all, lead her children to Jesus. That's what that mother did, and the Christian church and the world felt the impact of her son's faith and ministry. You can have that kind of impact too.

St. Paul is grateful when he remembers Timothy's sincere faith. Time and again Timothy had demonstrated that faith to Paul, on sunny and cloudy days, glad and sad days. That faith would stand firm, Paul was sure, because it had a good foundation. "Ever since you were a child you have known the Holy Scriptures," Paul wrote later in this letter, "which are able to give you the wisdom that leads to salvation through faith in Christ Jesus." Going on, "All Scripture is inspired by God," wrote Paul, "and is useful for teaching the truth, rebuking error, correcting faults, and giving instruction for right living" (2 Tim. 3:15-16 TEV). With that Scripture as his foundation, Timothy had learned the truth of God and the Spirit had brought him to faith.

And what a faith! It didn't shrink when faced with opposition, persecution, even death. That faith moved Timothy to be Paul's "right-hand man." Read through the Book of Acts and the letters of Paul, and you'll see what a prominent role this young man with the big faith had to play.

And where did it begin? With his mother Eunice and his grandmother Lois, who taught the little boy to pray a prayer that might have been our first prayer: "Abba, Father." That, dear friends, is the chief thing a mother can do: lead her child to Jesus.

We have a tendency to want to give our children more than we had: better clothing, more expensive toys and sports equipment, a better education. That's fine. But let's never forget the main thing we ought to do for them: lead them to Jesus.

We have to teach them about God and His great love and His plan of salvation. We have to teach them about Christ's great love in coming down to live among us, suffer and die a cruel death, and rise again. We have to teach them the mystery that can't be explained, that God is three yet one, and that we cannot believe unless the Holy Spirit comes to us through God's Word and sacraments. Never mind that you can't explain all this—you can't explain television, or electricity for that matter, or lightning, or the germination of a seed, or the birth of a baby—but that doesn't stop us from believing in those wondrous things. Just teach them, and the Spirit will do the rest.

What can a mother do?

Jesus said, "You can't have greater love than to give your life for your friends." Mothers know about that, instinctively. No one has to tell or teach them.

In August of 1980 terrorists attacked a synagogue in Vienna one sabbath day. As they burst into the room with machine guns and grenades, a mother threw herself down on her child to protect him. The child was spared, the mother was killed. You don't have to tell a mother why. . . .

Some years ago, on a farm in northeast Iowa, a mother heard a racket outside. She ran out to discover that her little toddler had climbed over the fence into the hogyard, and those big animals were going berserk. She didn't hesitate. She dashed to the fence, climbed over, picked up her little boy, and threw him to safety. But the crazed creatures, wild because they had little ones, knocked her down and mauled her so badly that she soon died. Mothers understand why she did that without hesitation, without thinking of her safety.

We admire that great love, and thank God for it. But it leads us to think of a love that's even greater. Is. 49:15 (TEV) says:

> So the Lord answers,
> "Can a woman forget her own baby
> and not love the child she bore?
> Even if a mother should forget her child,
> I will never forget you."

Even if a mother could forget her little baby (how unlikely that is!), even if that could happen, the Lord will *never* forget us. That's how much He loves us.

About 10 years ago the newspapers told about little Kathleen, age 11, who was knocked down by a high-voltage wire that had come loose in an accident. She was held there, dying. The other children were afraid to help, and they ran away. But little Jessica, age 9, didn't run. She came up to Kathleen, and although she got a bad shock herself, she managed to pull Kathleen free and save her life.

Our Lord Jesus didn't hesitate, either. He took hold of the high-voltage wire of sin that was killing all of us. He accepted its death-dealing charge into Himself. It killed Him, but He set us free! His cross and empty tomb are the guarantees of God's forgiveness and the sure hope of eternal life. That, dear mother, is the chief task you have. Lead them to know that Jesus.

What else can a mother do?

Oh, you have lots of opportunities. Let's look at a few of these glorious potentials you have:

1. You can teach your children how to make decisions. That, after all, is the main task of parenting. It's sad (I have seen it happen) when parents won't let go, when they feel they have to make all the decisions for their children, even though the children are old enough to be out from under parental control that may be repressive. Teach them, early on, to make God-pleasing decisions for themselves. That's not easy for parent or child, but it must be done for successful living.

2. Be a model of a happy, positive, God-fearing person. Children have so many negative models, so many anti-heroes. Show them someone who is creative, industrious, responsible. Use for your own model the noble women of the Bible, like Lois and Eunice, Sarah, Mary, the unnamed woman in Proverbs 31. Show your children the joy of responsibility; and remember, attitudes are caught, not taught.

3. Train your children in handling troubles. Show them that one alone carrying a burden has an almost impossible load, but two together can do it more easily. And one plus God is enough. Show them how you turn scars into stars! Show them you really believe that God loves us *all* the time.

4. Try to get them to set a good goal, and then go for it! When they reach that one, set another! That's not frustrating, it's exhilarating. You show them how.

5. Let them observe how you relate to an extended family in the body of Christ, the church, and in the world. Show them how you see yourself as a "neighbor" to other people. For instance, not every lady here today is a mother. Often we act as though everyone has to fit into a traditional family role where we have father-mother-children. Not so. We have single parents. We have single persons. We have elderly persons who are alone. Show your children how to relate to all of these, and that you see beauty and joy in each of them, and that your life is enriched as God leads you to share a smile with

them. (It wouldn't be a bad idea if you took a little time this afternoon and took the kids along with you to visit a lonely person in a home, perhaps a forgotten mother. Share part of your happy day with someone who doesn't have anyone!)

These are some of the potentials you have, but remember: Most of all, you want to lead your children to Jesus. That's the glorious opportunity God gives when He lets you become a parent.

Timothy turned out to be a mighty blessing for the church, in large part because his Christian mother did her joyful duty in bringing him up in God's discipline and instruction.

Someone asked the great jurist Oliver Wendell Holmes, "What is the secret of success?" Half in jest, he answered, "Choose the right parents." Of course we can't do that. God chooses our parents for us. Parents are gifts of God (and I personally can never thank God enough for my Christian parents; today I honor my mother, and express my gratitude to God for her). If we are parents, God has given us the gift of children. We can do no more, and no less, than live up to the responsibility that He gives, especially the opportunity to lead our children to Jesus. We can do this, with the help of His love and grace, in Christ our Savior. Amen.

Eugene F. Kramer

Related Scripture Readings

Prov. 31:10-31 John 2:1-11 Eph. 5:21-31

Suggested Hymns

"Children of the Heavenly Father"
"O Blest the House"
"Jesus! and Shall It Ever Be"

ORDINATION/INSTALLATION

The Office of the Ministry

COL. 4:17

Norman Vincent Peale, former pastor of Marble Collegiate Church in New York, nationally known author and lecturer, and often referred to as "the poor man's psychiatrist," relates that when he came to assume the pastorate of a church in Syracuse, N. Y., he was introduced to the congregation by his bishop as follows: "This is your new pastor. You can make of him a great man, or you can make him a very ordinary, mediocre individual. What the bishop was trying to tell the congregation, we believe, is quite obvious.

It is customary also in our Lutheran Church that the preacher on the occasion of the ordination (installation) of a pastor follow somewhat the same pattern. First, that he point out the duty of the congregation toward their pastor; second, that he point out the duty of the pastor toward the congregation. Today we are going to deviate from this tried and proven approach and, instead, simply share with you some thoughts on the office of the ministry.

The basis for our discourse is an exhortation written by the apostle Paul in his Letter to the Colossians to a man named Archippus (text). As far as we are able to determine, Archippus served first in the congregation at Ephesus and later in the congregation at Colossae as a presbyter or bishop. Some Bible scholars have, without sufficient grounds, construed the words of our text into a rebuke for past negligence. However, the historical aspects of our text are not our primary consideration today. Above all, we want to point out that the text emphatically states that the ministry is something received from God, and that after the office has been bestowed He expects it to be fulfilled. Also, the fulfillment of this office requires care, industry, devotion, consecration, and the application of every ability we can bring to it.

Perhaps the office of the ministry has never been so much misunderstood as in our day. James Robison in his book entitled *Adventurous Preaching* says: "The preacher once enjoyed a wide and uniquely central place in the life of our society. Time and progress have changed it radically. The place is still unique, but it is no longer central." There are few subjects on which error has been so frequent in the Christian church. I pray that today, under the guidance of God's Holy Spirit, we may express a few thoughts that will help dispel some of the fog by which the office of the ministry is too often surrounded.

First, what Scriptural basis do we have for the office of the ministry? We can answer that question without the slightest hesitation. The office of the ministry is a spiritual institution, ordained, appointed, taught, and commanded both directly and indirectly in the New Testament. Wherever the apostles founded churches, they appointed pastors to feed the flock they had gathered. In the Book of the Acts of the Apostles the doctrine is most lucidly expressed. If the two epistles of Paul to young Timothy and the one to Titus do not sanction the ministry, then words have no meaning. In Acts we read the broad fact that Paul "ordained elders in every church." Elders are mentioned six times in Acts and in the epistles of Peter and James. These and a mass of other facts undergird the office of the ministry as a Scriptural institution. Therefore never diminish or minimize the office the minister of Christ holds.

The ministerial office is an honorable privilege. What an honor it is to be an ambassador of the King of Kings! The person of an ambassador of state is respected and regarded as legally sacred. Before the invention of the telephone or even the telegraph, it was regarded as a highly coveted distinction to be the bearer of tidings of victory. How much greater an honor it is to be the ambassador proclaiming the good news of the victory achieved in Gethsemane, on Golgotha, and in Joseph's garden.

Great honors and privileges usually bring great responsibilities. The office of the ministry is also one of deep and painful responsibility. We watch for souls "as they that must give account" (Heb. 13:17 KJV). If all we would have to do is read services, administer sacraments, wear peculiar dress, and go through a round of rituals, our position would be comparatively easy. But this is not all. We have the responsibility of delivering our Master's message, keeping back nothing that is profitable, declaring all the counsel of God. If we tell our congregations less than the truth or more than the truth, we may endanger immortal souls.

We leave this phase of our subject with an earnest request that all who pray will never forget to make supplications, prayers, and intercessions for the ministers of Christ—and will pray that there may be a sufficient number of them, that they may be kept sound in the faith and holy in their lives, and that they may take heed to themselves as well as the doctrine (1 Tim. 4:16).

Next permit me to voice some cautions concerning the office of the ministry. There are some things that the minister is not and was never meant to be.

1. He is not a mediator between God and man. This is an office which belongs to Christ alone, and He never deputed it to anyone. Christianity is not a vicarious religion. By this we mean that no man can conceive of the church as an airplane, and once having occupied his seat on the plane he can quietly sit back and have the ecclesiastical jet engines fly him straight into heaven. This is a complete delusion. Every Christian must have personal dealing for himself with Christ, by his own faith, and no one else can act for him.

2. A minister cannot bestow grace. To give life is a prerogative of God, be that life physical or spiritual. "It is the Spirit that quickeneth" we read in John 6:63 (KJV). We may teach the value and need of grace, but we cannot give it. We may preach repentance, but we can go no further. What we say, the Holy Spirit must apply to the soul.

3. A minister is not infallible. The notion that a minister is absolutely immune to holding or teaching erroneous doctrine, and that we seldom need to doubt the truth of anything he says from the pulpit, is a comfortable but misleading error. Your ordination, dear brother, does not confer upon you immunity from error. Pastors, like congregations, may err both in living and in matters of faith. However noble the pastor's office may be, and however learned and devout he may appear, he is still only a man, a human being.

He can make mistakes. His opinion must never be valued above the Word of God.

The primary work for which the ministers of Christ are ordained and installed is to preach the Word. Our Lord during His public ministry was continually and everywhere a preacher. His last command to His apostles was "go into all the world and preach the Gospel to the whole creation" (Mark 16:15). In obedience to His command the apostles and disciples were continually preaching and teaching the Word. In Paul's last words to young Timothy he especially enjoins him to "preach the Word" (2 Tim. 4:2).

Church history bears out the importance of preaching. The shining hours of the early Christian church were those times when the golden-mouthed orator Chrysostom and the scholarly Augustine were constantly expounding God's Word. Conversely the darkest hours were those times just prior to the Reformation when the pulpit was silent and Christianity was reduced to a round of forms and rituals.

"Preach the Word." Your pulpit is to be the sounding board of the voice of almighty God ringing forth in clear trumpet tones that He "so loved the world that He gave His only begotten Son, that whosoever believeth in Him should not parish but have everlasting life" (John 3:16 KJV). If, brother, as you embark on your ministry here at ―――――――― there is anything that interferes with this primary task and duty, then shove it aside. There may be those who will say of you, "He can preach, but he can't do anything else." Forget such remarks, because generally speaking they will be unfounded. The preacher who can really preach must do something else, or he could not preach. No man can preach if he lives in an ivory tower. No man can preach if he loses contact with people. God has to have men in the pulpit—men who know how people are born, how they bark their shins, how they seer their souls, how they break their hearts, and how they die. Whenever the pulpit has ceased to give forth living water, drought and desert have spread over the earth. But when fountains have flowed from the pulpit, then the desert has become a garden and the fields of the heart have flowered.

However, even if God has placed it within your abilities to preach with the persuasion of a Dwight Moody, the profundity of a Henry Ward Beecher, the rhetorical beauty of a Phillips Brooks, and the conviction of a Charles Haddon Spurgeon, and you do not dwell upon the one great central truth of all Christianity, then your preaching will be "as sounding brass or a tinkling cymbal" (1 Cor. 13:1 KJV). That one great central truth of Christianity, that one theme which you dare never forsake if you would serve God and man, is Christ and Him crucified.

David Susskind, in an article entitled "The Millennium of the Mental Midgets," wrote: "Today in our churches we find in the pulpit men whose sole talent is knowing how to put a wet finger into the wind to see how the zephyrs of public attitude are blowing so that they can appeal to as many people as possible." Needless to say, this wet-finger-in-the-wind is worlds apart from the "Thus saith the Lord" of the true prophet. Too often considerations of his own security hinder the preacher from proclaiming the Word of the Lord. Thus he is leading his people back to the fleshpots of Egypt rather than forward to the Promised Land. He has become the priest of the comfort cult, which has as its slogan "Give me security or give me death." What a contrast to the battle cry of the prophet of another generation: "Move forward, and the Lord will go before you."

There comes a time in the life of every preacher when he is sorely tempted to broaden his horizon of preaching. He feels that if he would not confine himself so much to the Bible and to the Bible only, then perhaps he could hold the attention of his hearers to a far greater degree. A young pastor who had been in office less than a year once approached a veteran of the cross with this question: "Is it necessary for me to preach from the Bible every Sunday? Soon there will be nothing new in what I say, and my sermons will become a threadbare tale too often told." The reply of the wise and aged pastor was somewhat as follows: "Fly on, little bird, until your wings drop off and your tailfeathers vanish, and you will never exhaust the air; swim on, little fish, until your fins drop off and your tail drops off, and you will never exhaust the water; preach on, young man, until your eyes become dim and your voice is lost in a whisper, and you will never exhaust the beauties of the blessed truths of Holy Scripture."

Our sin-sick world has to hear about Christ again, and again, and again. In your preaching tell your hearers about the atonement Christ made by His death, His vicarious sacrifice on the cross, the redemption He obtained for all humanity by His blood, His victory over death by His resurrection, His active life of intercession at God's right hand, and the absolute necessity of simple faith in Him. Preach that message, and you can with confidence and assurance preach from this pulpit or any pulpit, because you know that what you have to say transcends the dichotomy of mind and body, body and soul, heaven and earth, day and night, and even time and eternity.

There are yet many things we would say to you and the members of the congregation as you now become overseer of the flock in this section of the Lord's vineyard, but time does not permit. Therefore we commend you and the members of the flock to the providence of an eternal, almighty heavenly Father, to the guidance of an ever-present Holy Spirit, and to the limitless love of an all-sufficient Savior with this prayer on your lips:

> Lord Jesus, I have promised to serve Thee to the end;
> Be Thou forever near me, my Master and my Friend.
> I shall not fear the battle if Thou art by my side,
> Nor wander from the pathway if Thou wilt be my guide.
>
> O Jesus, Thou hast promised to all who follow Thee,
> That where Thou art in glory, there shall Thy servant be;

And Jesus, I have promised to serve Thee to the end;
O give me grace to follow, my Master and my Friend.

Otto W. Toelke

Related Scripture Readings

Ps. 37:5
Is. 21:6
Is. 52:7-10
Matt. 28:19
Rom. 1:16

Suggested Hymns

"All Hail the Power of Jesus' Name"
"Jesus, Jesus, Only Jesus"
"Dear Lord, to Thy True Servants Give"
"We Bid Thee Welcome in the Name"
"Lord of the Church, We Humbly Pray"
"Pour Out Thy Spirit from on High"
"Send, O Lord, Thy Holy Spirit"

RALLY DAY

Caleb's Rally Day Sermon for Our Day

NUM. 13:30

From your Sunday school lessons most of you have heard of Moses. Quite probably you can recall Joshua. But we do not hear much about Caleb, the companion of Moses and Joshua.

On this our Sunday school Rally Day it is well for us to recall Caleb, because he preached one of the earliest Rally Day sermons on record. Caleb's sermon is appropriate for us today as we resolve to rally around our Lord and His church once again to renew our efforts through our Sunday school to reach out to people with the Word of God.

Caleb's sermon is short and simple. We read only this: "But Caleb quieted the people before Moses, and said, "Let us go up at once, and occupy it; for we are well able to overcome it.' "

Caleb's Rally Day Sermon for Our Day

I. Its Challenge

The first thing we note in Caleb's sermon is the challenge that Caleb presented to ancient Israel—and to us.

You will recall how God through Moses delivered the Israelites from a life of slavery in Egypt to one of freedom. He promised to lead this people to a promised land, Canaan, "flowing with milk and honey." God kept His promise. After leading them for a year or two, the Lord brought His people to the southern boundary of the land He had promised them. He now urged the Israelites to enter and to occupy this land for themselves and for their children.

To prepare themselves for taking over this land, the Israelites sent 12 spies, one from each tribe of Israel, to "get the lay of the land." They were to seek information about the strength and number of its inhabitants, the fertility and productivity of the soil, the fortifications of the cities, the culture of the people, and other useful information.

Upon their return the spies reported that the Lord had indeed told them the truth—Canaan was certainly a land "flowing with milk and honey." They brought with them grapes and other products to show their countrymen just how rich and productive Canaan was. But they also had discouraging words: "Yet the people who dwell in the land are strong, and the cities are fortified and very large; and besides, we saw the descendants of Anak there" (Num. 13:28). To these fearful spies the inhabitants seemed to be as giants and the Israelites as but grasshoppers in their sight.

Having heard the report of the 10 false spies, the Israelites lost heart and clamored to return to Egypt rather than perish in this unknown land to which they had been brought.

In this situation of despair Caleb stilled the commotion and rallied God's people with the stirring words: "Let us go up at once, and occupy it; for we are well able to overcome it."

Our situation today is quite similar to that of Israel on this occasion. The Lord has done great things for us. In His time the Father sent His Son, Jesus Christ, into our world to keep God's law in our stead and to endure the divine punishment for our sins in our behalf. He did this to deliver us from the slavery of sin and death, and to bring us into the promised land of His kingdom. The Holy Spirit has called us individually into the company of God's people so that we can experience for ourselves the fruits of Christ's saving work. The Spirit has given us the high dignity of being His representatives in the world. As such we are to share with all people the glorious Gospel of the eternal salvation gained for us by Jesus Christ, our Savior. Our Sunday school exists to teach God's people in our midst what it means to be a Christian and to equip one another to live as God's representatives in the everyday world. Our Sunday school also seeks to reach out to all people in our community who do not know the salvation Christ has gained for them and to share the Good News with them.

But we too must face great obstacles that would discourage us. The world itself lies in the power of the evil one (1 John 5:19). By nature all people prefer to serve evil rather than God. People dismiss goodness and righteousness as "namby-pamby Sunday school stuff." Those who seek to serve God by loving their fellow human beings are frequently ridiculed as being naive "pushovers." Just because the world is in the power of the evil one, it scorns those who would speak for God and walk in His ways.

The spirit of our times is set against the Gospel of Jesus Christ. Our generation has been termed "the now generation," "the me generation." People are not interested in the future, particularly in eternity. So many are concerned only about themselves. They do not want to hear that they are responsible to God for the way they live. They want to feel that they are O.K. just as they are. They do not want to be reminded that by nature they are under the judgment of God and are in need of a Savior. Blinding themselves to their responsibility to God, people by-and-large do not want to be told that God expects them to serve Him by accepting responsibility for their fellow human beings everywhere. They want to live only for themselves. We can readily understand why so many people do not want Sunday school. What is taught there would disturb their entire way of life.

Then there are the many people baptized in our churches who perhaps did go to Sunday school for a few years. It is discouraging to note how many people have given up the church and Sunday school for the world and its evil. Never before in the history of our nation has there been such widespread apostasy as during the past 15 years. For example, and this is typical of most Christian denominations, of all children baptized in our church body during the past 15 years, less than half are enrolled in one of our Sunday schools. More than 40 percent of the infants baptized in our congregations are never confirmed. As we observe such widespread rejection of the Sunday school and the Gospel that is taught in it, we can easily become discouraged and lose interest.

To stir up our enthusiasm and to rally us together to meet the great challenges of today's world, Caleb would say to us as he did to God's people of old: "Let us go up at once, and occupy it; for we are well able to overcome it."

II. Its Promise

The second thing we hear in Caleb's stirring Rally Day sermon is its note of confidence: "Let us go up at once, and occupy it; *for we are well able to overcome it.*"

What was it that made Caleb so confident? He knew that it was the Lord who had brought the Israelites out of the slavery of Egypt. He had observed the Lord's many miracles through which He had provided for the needs of His people. He had heard the Lord's command to enter the Promised Land, and He believed God's promise that He would go with them to bless them.

We too have sound reasons for being confident as we rally together to work with the Lord during this coming season in our Sunday school. We have God's command: "Make disciples of all nations, baptizing them in the name of the Father and of the Son and of the Holy Spirit, teaching them to observe all that I have commanded you." And we also have God's promise: "Lo, I am with you always, to the close of the age" (Matt. 28:19-20).

As we in our Sunday school teach the Word of the Lord, we are never alone. Our Lord Jesus Christ, before He ascended into heaven, promised to send the Holy Spirit to teach us all things and to bring to our remembrance all that He taught while on earth (John 14:26). The Holy Spirit is ever with us as we teach the Word of God, to awaken and sustain faith and to empower us to live as God would have us live.

We can be confident not only because we have the Gospel of Jesus Christ, through which the Holy Spirit works, but also because the Holy Spirit gives us people with talents sufficient for our task. We may not always realize this; we may complain that it is difficult to find people willing to teach. But we have been given these people nevertheless. We need but identify them and enlist them for the great work of teaching. We to whom the Spirit has given talents for teaching need but to come forward and place ourselves in God's service through teaching in our Sunday school.

So on this Rally Day we face the future of our Sunday school with confidence as we say with Caleb: "Let us go up at once, and occupy it; for we are well able to overcome it."

III. Its Sense of Urgency

The third point we note in Caleb's Rally Day sermon is his sense of urgency: "Let us go up *at once.*"

Caleb recognized that "for everything there is a season, and a time for every matter under heaven" (Eccl. 3:1).

Now was God's time for His people to occupy the Promised Land. Should they pass up this opportunity at this time, who knew when they would have the opportunity again?

Caleb was right in being urgent. The Israelites did reject his plea, and refused to enter Canaan. As a result the 10 false spies died from a plague from the Lord, and all Israelites 20 years old and over were condemned to wander 40 years in the wilderness without ever reaching their destination.

Finally, having realized the consequences of their refusal, the Israelites changed their minds and subsequently offered to enter Canaan after all. But then it was too late. Moses warned the people that through their unbelief they had forfeited God's promise to go with them. Should they now enter Canaan, they would only be defeated by the Canaanites and the Amalekites. The people persisted and attempted to go into Canaan. They were met by the Amalekites and Canaanites—and were utterly defeated. God's opportunity for them had come and gone; now it was too late.

With the same sense of urgency Caleb would urge us today to rally together and meet our opportunities "at once." Tomorrow, next year, may be too late.

Are all of us making use of today's opportunities to study the Word of God in our Sunday school? Are we sharing our talents for teaching the Word? Are we reaching out to the unchurched people in our community? Are we making use of every opportunity to grow in our personal Christian faith and life and to share with others the Gospel of the world's only Savior? As St. Paul wrote: "Working together with Him, then, we entreat you not to accept the grace of God in vain. For He says, 'At the acceptable time I have listened to you, and helped you on the day of salvation.' Behold, now is the acceptable time; behold, now is the day of salvation" (2 Cor. 6:1-2).

As we view our opportunities and review our trust in God's promises, "let us go up at once, and occupy it; for we are well able to overcome it."

Dale E. Griffin

Related Scripture Readings

Num. 13:16-14:45	Matt. 16:24-28	Heb. 3:7-19
Matt. 11:25-30	Matt. 18:1-5, 10-14	Heb. 4:1-11

Suggested Hymns

"My God, Accept My Heart This Day"
"Renew Me, O Eternal Light"
"Stand Up! Stand Up for Jesus"
"Rise, Ye Children of Salvation"
"Soldiers of the Cross, Arise"
"Savior, Who Thy Flock Art Feeding"

STEWARDSHIP

"Now Concerning the Collection . . ."

1 COR. 16:1-2

In Christ Jesus, dear friends. It has been said that generalities are for weak minds, and I will not insult you with generalities. I will be very specific this morning. Paul certainly was specific when he wrote his letters to the Corinthians. Paul was direct, he was blunt, he set forth a simple plan for giving for worthy Christian service. He immediately got down to *brass tacks.*

Most of you are familiar with 1 Corinthians 13. This great "love chapter" in the New Testament says, in effect: "Things go better with love."

Paul's First Letter to the Corinthians is the story of how Paul met the problems of a problem-child congregation. Today read through 1 Corinthians in your Bible. You'll find almost every kind of problem that can face a congregation. By the time the 15th chapter is reached, Paul speaks to those who denied the resurrection, or watered it down to a mere immortality of the soul.

Let's look at the context surrounding Paul's great passage on giving. 1 Cor. 15:1-2: "The Gospel . . . by which you are saved." 15:3: "Christ died for our sins." 15:4: "He was buried . . . was raised on the third day." 15:20: "Christ has been raised from the dead." This almost sounds like the Apostles' Creed. This is 1 Cor. 15:51: "Lo! I tell you a mystery. We shall not all sleep, but we shall all be changed." 15:54, right through to the end: "Then shall come to pass the saying that is written: 'Death is swallowed up in victory.' 'O death, where is thy victory? O death, where is thy sting?' The sting of death is sin, and the power of sin is the Law. But thanks be to God, who gives us the victory through our Lord Jesus Christ. Therefore, my beloved brethren, be steadfast, immovable, always abounding in the work of the Lord, knowing that in the Lord your labor is not in vain."

Now, as I am quoting Scripture, please remember there were no chapter divisions, no verses. Paul just kept on going. So after this great chapter on the resurrection and those great words that we are to abound in the work of the Lord, he continues. The next line says: *"Now concerning the collection . . ." (KJV).* He takes no time in 1 Cor. 16:1 to spell out precisely what is involved in our giving. He moves to 16:2 (KJV): *When?*—"Upon the first day of the week." *Who?*—"Let every one of you." *What?*—"Lay by him in store." *How much?*—"As God hath prospered him."

Putting it in simple words, Paul was saying: *Regular giving.* Everybody is to give. Even as each one must believe for himself to be saved, so each one's faith will prove itself by his own giving. Our giving (v. 3) should be systematic. Whenever one has income, take out the Lord's share first and lay it aside. Lay aside a definite, generous percentage of your income for the Lord. That is a starting point in your giving. Let your love for Jesus and your further ability to give move you to go beyond that starting point. Start with a certain percentage, but don't stop there.

Now, what happened after Paul wrote to the people of Corinth? The three responses sound almost like a typical congregation of today. (1) They readily agreed to meet the appeal; (2) they did make a beginning; (3) they failed to contribute what Paul considered an adequate amount of money.

Before we go any further, let me remind you that Christ has much to say about your money and what you do with it. You work for 40, 50, 60 hours a week. You give your imagination, your sweat, your labor, your ingenuity, your education, your experience, your background. All for a piece of paper saying "so much money." Or for the hope that your efforts will bear fruit and bring in money. In other words, you trade yourself in for money.

When you remember that God owns what you have traded yourself in for, including money, then you realize that you are His by right of creation.

But does God really own you? He certainly does! He is the Creator of heaven and earth, of all things visible and invisible. Ps. 24:1 says: "The earth is the Lord's and the fullness thereof, the world and those who dwell therein." You are His by right of creation.

Since Jesus Christ has redeemed us, purchased us, and won us—bought us back—with His precious blood, we are His. We are His by right of redemption.

In those who call upon the Lord, the Holy Spirit has worked faith through the preaching of the Word and through the sacraments. So they have become heirs of eternal life and are His by right of sanctification.

You trade yourself in for money. You are not your own. You are God's. You either have to give up all that you have to Christ, who bought you, or you have to be a thief and keep what is not yours. So Christ has not only something, but everything, to say about your money. *It is His!*

What does He say? Look in 2 Cor. 5:15: "He died for all, that those who live might live no longer for themselves but for Him who for their sake died and was raised." There you have it . . . the purpose of living is giving—giving one's self to Christ.

Let us look at our own congregation's program of Mission and Ministry for the coming year. Our financial goals, as a congregation call for $ ——— to be given by the members of this parish. And so, as with the Christians at Corinth: (1) We have agreed to meet the appeal; (2) we have made a beginning; (3) now will we contribute what would be considered an adequate amount of money?

Adequate by whose standards? We ourselves have been setting programs of work. We set the program in light of the work the Lord has set before us, in view of our wishes and capabilities.

The question is not whether this is what you are going to give, because you do not give to a budget. You give to God, from what He has given to you. So a question bigger than, "What needs to be done?" is the question, "How has God blessed me?"

God does not ask that we give from what we don't have, but from what we do have. Our giving is not limited to needs you know and see. Our giving is limited by what God has given to us.

When Paul saw that the Corinthians were slipping, he did not simply say, "I think they are heading for failure." Nor did Paul simply resign himself to the level of interest in giving that satisfied the Corinthians.

Paul came back in his Second Letter with another appeal. He kept the message of God in front of them lest they forget. Paul felt it was not only his right but his duty to challenge their liberality. He says, that we should grow in this grace also.

Paul's first appeal was only 4 verses long. His second was 39 verses, covering the entire eighth and ninth chapters of Second Corinthians. In this

Second Letter he shared the example of liberality of the church in Macedonia.

Listen as he contrasts these churches. The Macedonians gave according to their means, and beyond, of their own free will. You Corinthians didn't. The Macedonians begged for the privilege of taking part in the relief of the saints. You Corinthians did not. The Macedonians did it not as we expected, but first they gave themselves to the Lord. You Corinthians did not (2 Cor. 8:1-5). Paul praises the Corinthians for their present spiritual fruits and urges them to bring forth also the grace of liberality. "You are so rich in all you have: in faith, speech, and knowledge, in your eagerness to help and in your love for us. And so we want you to be generous also in this service of love" (2 Cor. 8:7 TEV). Lest anyone misunderstand, Paul carefully states his intentions. The Corinthians are to prove, as the Macedonians did, that their love for Christ is genuine.

He reinforces this opportunity with a restatement of Christ's mission and ministry. Christ became poor that they might be enriched. Let them become poor if necessary, that like their Lord they may enrich others. That is what giving is all about.

But! Here comes the eternal "but"—"but I have to care for my family" . . . "but my salary is not high" . . . "but I'm so young or so old" . . . "but" . . . "but" . . . "but" . . .

Paul anticipates and removes all excuses when he counsels everyone to give according to the measure of his ability. "As God hath prospered him" (KJV). Or, as Paul says in 2 Cor. 8:12, we should give according to our means. Provided there is an eager desire to give, God accepts "what a man has." He does not ask for "what he has not." In 2 Cor. 9:11 (TEV) we hear: "He will always make you rich enough to be generous at all times." Strong words? Maybe.

Can you imagine a church board receiving such a letter as Paul wrote to Corinth? Or a church member receiving this type of a letter from his pastor? Perhaps we lack the grace to receive such a letter as the Corinthians received it.

Someone has suggested an offering prayer like this as our offerings are brought to the Lord's altar: "Dear Lord, after all we say or do, this is really what we think of You!"

Really, our giving becomes kind of a test of our life. Let me illustrate: In deciding what to give, do you think in terms of the high cost of living rather than the blessings that God has poured out on your family? Frankly, often *we confuse the high cost of living with the cost of living high.*

A story tells of a 10-year-old boy who came to his dad for money to buy him a birthday present. When the son buys Dad a tie with Dad's money and gives it to Dad, Dad still says "thank you." That's fine, but we shouldn't lose sight of whose money it was. So with God in our giving. Who is giving anyway? It is God's money. Thus the fair share in Christian stewardship and worship is not a certain percentage or a certain number of dollars. The "fair share" is the whole share.

Some like to say, "What I give is between God and me." That's a pleasant half-truth, but Christian giving is more than a private affair. It can be not only a confession of faith but a joyous act of worship. It shows concern for our brothers and sisters, both those in the faith and those who have not learned that Jesus is their Savior. The overpowering motive for my giving is God's giving. God gives so we can.

And so in our worship the offering follows the offertory. We sing, "Create in me a clean heart, O God"; then we worship the Lord with our gifts. There is a reason: We worship God with our hearts and with our hands and our voices . . . with all of our life. Proportionate giving is what our text is asking for; that is what God asks. Certainly it is not giving the average. Take the word proportion apart. It is the "portion for" and whom is the "portion for"? The Lord. When love and sacrifice combine, the tithe is a good precedent, but don't press the precedent and make a rule out of it.

Love never seeks a bargain. How should you determine God's portion? First, seek His will for you. Talk it over with God in prayer. Look at the true needs of His cause, and seek counsel of good stewards. Then listen to the words of 2 Cor. 8:9: "You know the grace of our Lord." God's pledges are written where we can see and read them. They are reliable, for they have all been certified by the resurrection of His Son. They are verified by Christian experience and tested by Christian faith. You know the grace of our Lord Jesus Christ. Prove the sincerity of your love.

The hymn writer put it this way: "Were the whole realm of nature mine,/ that were a tribute far too small;/ love so amazing, so divine,/ demands my soul, my life, my all!" Amen.

Marcus T. Zill

Related Scripture Readings

1 Kings 17:8-16
Luke 21:1-4
2 Cor. 8:1-15
Mark 12:41-44
Rom. 11:33-36

Suggested Hymns

"Forgive Us, Lord, for Shallow Thankfulness"
"Lord of Glory, You Have Bought Us"
"Praise and Thanksgiving"
"We Give You but Your Own"
"Take My Life, O Lord, Renew"
("Take My Life that It May Be")

THANKSGIVING

Are You Thankful? Prove It

PS. 107:2a

It's Thanksgiving Day! Ever since the time of President Lincoln, each president of our country has issued a call to the citizens of our land to give thanks to God. This year our President has again issued his Thanksgiving Proclamation. Back in Old Testament days a thanksgiving proclamation was issued by the writer of the 107th Psalm. In this general call to all people everywhere he calls out: "O give thanks to the Lord, for He is good; for His steadfast love endures forever!" (v. 1). At the beginning of this call for thanksgiving he tells us of the mercy and loving-kindness of God. Four times throughout the psalm the writer repeats the statement: "Let them thank the Lord for His enduring love" (vv. 8, 15, 21, 31) each time identifying how God's loving-kindness is responsible for specific blessings.

Today we would like to pause in the midst of our daily activities to reflect on the many blessings that have come our way, so that we too might speak out and express our thankfulness. This is what our text encourages us to do as it says: "Let the redeemed of the Lord say so." To assist us as we think of our blessings, I would like to put my topic in the form of a question:

Are You Thankful? Prove It

I. God Gave You Life

One of the great blessings that we experience each day, and which we so often take for granted, is the gift of life. Day after day we pick up our newspapers and read reports of people who have died. Yet here we are today, and we are very much alive. Is it because of the careful life-style we have adopted? Are we here because of the giant strides that have been made in medical science? Or are we experiencing life today because we are "lucky" and our time has not yet come? Martin Luther gives us the secret of our life in his explanation of the First Article of the Creed, as he says: "God has made me and all creatures; He has given me my body and soul, eyes, ears, and all my members . . . and still preserves them; He richly and daily provides me with all that I need to support this body and life." Here is reason number one for being thankful today. God has given me my life, and He preserves that life and provides what I need for that life. It has been said that we are only one heartbeat away from eternity. That is true. And it is God who controls every one of those heartbeats.

Are you thankful for your life? Then prove it. Take care of your life;

don't waste it. Don't be careless with your life. Perhaps one of the most glaring evidences of the misuse of life is the carelessness, the negligence, and the downright lack of concern that has led to more than 100,000 deaths last year and 10 million serious injuries that were caused by accidents that could have been prevented. What a waste of the wonderful gift of life which God has given!

The violence that occurs in our society, the deliberate disregard for the sacredness of life, the willful hurts that are inflicted on others because of jealousy, selfishness, and greed—all give evidence that many people have forgotten or never knew that life is precious. It is the gift of God.

Our gratitude for God's gift of life should become even greater when we remember that our life is experienced in a world filled with wonder and beauty. King David once exclaimed: "The heavens are telling the glory of God; and the firmament proclaims His handiwork" (Ps. 19:1). The very part of this wonderful world in which we have the privilege to live—the United States—especially offers us exciting opportunities for "life, liberty, and the pursuit of happiness." Here we can secure an education, seek employment, enjoy the benefits of excellent health facilities, and take full advantage of the right to worship God according to the dictates of our conscience.

How wonderfully God enriches our life by granting blessings each day. He doesn't give His blessings all at one time and then deprive us of them. No. Daily He gives food and clothing, shelter and home, family and friends, peace, health, and hundreds of other blessings—not because we have in any way merited or deserved them, but because of "His steadfast love." No wonder the psalmist prods us as he says, "Let the redeemed of the Lord say so." Speak up! Are you thankful?—Prove it!

II. God Gave You Spiritual Life

While the psalm speaks of "the redeemed" as people who have been delivered from distress when they cried to the Lord, it is most important that we remember that God has not only provided temporal deliverance; He has given eternal deliverance through His Son Jesus Christ, our Lord. From our confirmation instruction days, we in the Lutheran Church have understood the word "redeemed" to mean that Christ has bought us back from the power of sin, death, and the devil because He paid the price for our salvation. Luther reminds us of this also when he writes in his explanation of the Second Article of the Creed: "I believe that Jesus Christ . . . has redeemed me, a lost and condemned creature, purchased and won me from all sin, from death, and from the power of the devil; not with gold or silver, but with His holy, precious blood and with His innocent suffering and death, that I may be His own, and live under Him in His kingdom, and serve Him in everlasting righteousness, innocence, and blessedness."

Recognition of Christ and the salvation we have through Him means that we have more than mere life—we have everlasting life, and that calls for real thanksgiving. The Gospel for this day reminds us of the "thankful Samaritan," the one lone leper who returned to give thanks to Christ. Remember, of the ten men who were healed from the dread disease of leprosy, only one was thankful and proved it. Have you ever thought that his expression of gratitude occurred because he knew who had healed him? He really knew and believed in Jesus. The others didn't really know Christ as the Source of all blessings. That is why they didn't bother to come back to Him. That is the basic reason why many fail to give thanks today. It is not that they merely forget and thoughtlessly overlook the importance of giving thanks. It's because they don't really know Jesus as Lord and Savior. If they did, they would "say so."

Because many fail to prove their thankfulness, they forfeit additional blessings that could be theirs by God's grace. Take note of the fact that the "thankful Samaritan" not only went home in excellent physical condition; he went home "whole." Spiritual health and the fulness of God's grace were his.

Are you thankful for the spiritual deliverance secured for you by God's own Son, your Savior? Then prove it. Luther suggests that we can prove our thankfulness by "living under Christ in His kingdom" and by "serving Him in everlasting righteousness, innocence, and blessedness" (Second Article). St. Paul puts it very plainly as he says to the Corinthian Christians that Christ "died for all, that those who live might live no longer for themselves but for Him who for their sake died and was raised" (2 Cor. 5:15).

"Let the redeemed of the Lord say so." If there was ever a time when we needed to acknowledge God's goodness in granting us new life in Christ, it is now. As society moves into the rapidly passing years of this century, the wave of indifference and opposition to revealed religion seems to grow more serious. Only one thing can stop the flood of evil, and that is genuine thankfulness that grows out of an awareness of Jesus Christ as Lord and Savior. Within a few weeks we will enter the joyous Advent season, at which time we will reflect on Christ's initial coming into our world to be our Savior, and His final coming at the end of time to claim His own. That Christ, "the Author and Finisher of our faith" (Heb. 12:2 KJV), must be at the center of our Thanksgiving today. The plea of the psalmist must strike a responsive chord in our heart. "Let the redeemed of the Lord say so."

III. God Gives You Opportunities to Serve

Thankfulness on this day must not only be evidenced because God has given us life here, and in addition has given us the assurance of eternal life in the world to come, but also because He has given us exciting opportunities each day to engage in Christian service activities. Unfortunately, many of us are more concerned about what we can get and receive than what we can give. We rejoice when others do for us, but forget about what we can do for others.

The Third Article of our Christian creed speaks about the work of the Holy Spirit which we call sanctification. This has to do with the new life we live in Christ, and the ministry we carry out in His name. I like to think about the brief but enlightening message that Jesus presented in the synagogue in Nazareth at the beginning of His public ministry as He read from the Scriptures: "The Spirit of the Lord is upon Me, because He has anointed Me to preach good news to the poor. He has sent Me to proclaim release to the captives and recovering of sight to the blind, to set at liberty those who are oppressed" (Luke 4:18). As He closed the Scriptures, He said: "Today this scripture has been fulfilled in your hearing" (v. 21). Notice that Jesus speaks of the Holy Spirit anointing Him for a life of service. This is God's will for each one of us—that the Holy Spirit might empower us to become involved in serving each other and in reaching out to those who are in need of our help. That is why God has "called us by the Gospel and enlightened us with His gifts." Not that we might be self-serving, but so that we might reflect God's love in works of mercy toward others. We have been saved to serve. As Jesus came to serve, so He calls us through the Holy Spirit to serve. And thank God for the unlimited opportunities He gives us!

We live in a world where hunger and poverty claim the lives of about five million people a year, where malnutrition affects the lives of more than 700 million. Every 30 seconds 100 children are born in the developing countries of the world. Twenty of them will die within a year. Of the 80 who survive, 60 will have no access to modern medical care during their childhood. An equal number will suffer from malnutrition during their crucial early years, with the possibility of serious physical and mental damage. There will be no educational opportunities for more than 300 million of these children. On this day so many Americans will stuff themselves with turkey and all the fixings. It is well to remember the millions who don't know what a roast turkey looks like, but instead are thankful if they have a cup of wheat, a measure of corn, or a bowl of rice that can be flavored with a few scraps of pork.

I am not telling you of the poverty and hunger in our world to make you feel guilty because you have so much, but to remind you that through our church's World Relief and Social Service programs God gives us opportunities to serve others in Jesus' name.

Families in our communities that may be experiencing difficulties due to sickness, unemployment, parent/child relationships, or other pressures of daily living need our help, not only through a special Thanksgiving basket but through our ongoing prayers, our continuing concern, and our caring support. The Bible says: "As we have opportunity, let us do good unto all men and especially to those who are of the household of faith" (Gal. 6:10).

Our congregation on this day is being given another opportunity to permit God the Holy Spirit to really make us a "caring congregation," one that is sensitive to the needs and problems of people, and then to reach out in loving service and concern. This is what Jesus was talking about on the night before Good Friday as He said to His disciples: "A new commandment I give to you, that you love one another; even as I have loved you, that you also love one another. By this all men will know that you are My disciples, if you have love for one another" (John 13:34-35). Thank God today and every day for the opportunities we have to demonstrate our love for our Savior by serving His redeemed people.

A little congregation was surprised at the close of a very inspiring service. They had heard the praises of God sung by the choir; they had listened to the appropriate Scripture lessons; they had joined in the faith strengthening hymns and had listened carefully to the pastor's sermon. The surprise came after the benediction when the members turned to leave the church. A large banner had been unfurled over the exit doors which read: "You have heard the Word—now go and serve." Service was to be the follow-up of the worship. They had heard the Gospel of God's love in Christ; now they were to put that good news into practice. For this opportunity they would also be thankful.

"Let the redeemed of the Lord say so." Yes, let the reality of our thankfulness be seen. Speak your thanks, live your thanks, and share your thanks! Amen.

Leslie F. Weber

Related Scripture Readings

Deut. 8:1-20 Luke 17:11-19 1 Tim. 2:1-4

Suggested Hymns

"Come, Ye Thankful People, Come"
"Praise to God, Immortal Praise"
"We Praise Thee, O God"
"Now Thank We All Our God"

WEDDING

Who's Boss in Your Household?

EPH. 5:21-33

We live in an age of rights: civil rights, women's rights, workers' rights. People are concerned about equality and fairness: in politics, in the marketplace, and in the home.

What about your home? Who's the boss? Who's in charge? Who's got the upper hand of rights and privileges?

A wedding ceremony is a joyous occasion to celebrate the uniting of a husband and wife. It is a time of reflection, too. It is a time when we pause from the frantic preparations that accompany the beginning of married life in today's society. The wedding ceremony is, above all, a time to reflect on what the Lord says about this institution called marriage.

God placed the first man and woman together. Adam and Eve had much more than a garden apartment—they had a whole garden, the Garden of Eden. God placed the man in the garden, and Eve was placed by his side. What a beautiful household it was! Not even a hassle about who was in charge—yet.

Apparently, it had never occured to Adam and Eve that they would have to seek out their rights and privileges in their garden household. They never argued about who would pay the bills or whose name would appear first on the checkbook. Life just wasn't that complicated—yet.

Apparently, Adam and Eve didn't have to fight about who was going to be the boss in their household. They weren't faced with the decision of who would wear the pants in their family. In fact, no one wore pants in their family—yet.

Rights and privileges were thoughts that hadn't occurred to Adam and Eve, God's first bride and groom. It seemed fine to them that God had charge of their garden household; He seemed to do a pretty good job, too! Adam and Eve were in love with each other, and they loved the Lord their God. They walked with Him and talked with Him. They were a happy household in the garden. However, the honeymoon was about to end.

Enter the serpent. With the serpent, sin entered the household of God's first bride and groom. The temptation was the opportunity for full rights and privileges. The temptation was to be like God. The temptation was to be boss.

Since that day mankind has been interested in rights and privileges. The idea of submission is not very popular!

Yet this is exactly what St. Paul writes about in Eph. 5:21-33. In an age in which so many people look for their privileges, the Bible reminds us of our responsibilities. Scripture speaks of our submission to one another and our reverence for the Lord.

St. Paul says that wives should submit themselves to their husbands. He says that husbands do have authority over their wives. The problem that most people have with that statement comes from looking at the concept of submission from the wrong end. Yes, wives are to submit to their husbands. However, is that only a statement of a husband's privilege over his wife? No way! The wife is to submit to her husband the way the church submits to the authority of Christ.

God's people do not submit to Christ by force or grudgingly. Our submission to Jesus Christ is an act of love. It is, in fact, our response to Him who already loved us.

God knows all about the responsibilities of love. John 3:16 says that God loved the world so much that He gave His Son. Jesus Christ went all the way to the cross and the grave as an expression of His love. The sin that has split up households since Adam and Eve is taken away by the forgiveness of the Cross. Jesus shed His blood so that the sins of self-centeredness would no longer rule in the household and in the hearts of those who live there. Jesus understood very well His responsibility to mankind. Jesus spoke the powerful words of love in John 15:13: "Greater love has no man than this, that a man lay down his life for his friends."

Through His death on the cross Jesus Christ brings us into union with our Creator. He gives us new life. He frees us—to be the people He has called us to be. We are freed to be God's people—in the world, in the marketplace, and in the household. We are freed to live as husbands and wives who look at marriage not from the perspective of privileges but from the viewpoint of responsibilities.

St. Paul talks of submission. Wives are to submit to their husbands in the same way that the church submits to Christ: Not because it has to but because it wants to! Not under the tyranny of the Law but under the freedom of the Gospel. Husbands are to love their wives in the same way Christ loves His people, the church: Not because He had to but because He wanted to! Not under the demand of rules but with the unending love that cost Him His life at Calvary.

The good news is that God's love has penetrated this world. Satan couldn't stop it. Sin couldn't sidetrack it. The cross couldn't roadblock it. Even the grave could not deter the love of God that is in Christ Jesus. The victory of the Resurrection is a victory for every household. It is the victory of God's love that enables us to submit ourselves to one another and to the Lord Jesus Christ.

On their wedding day most couples receive a lot of beautiful gifts. However, the most precious gift of all is the victorious presence of Jesus Christ. He is present in the hearts and lives of Christians; and when those Christians marry, He is present in their household.

Jesus Christ is present not just in theory but in a real, concrete way. The Lord is not just an ancient friend out of a page in history. He is the living Lord who is present in concrete ways—the Word and the sacraments. These are the ways Christ works in the lives of the bride and groom who submit to Him.

When Jesus Christ is boss, when the Lord is the Head of the household, His Word is the foundation for the family. The household that submits to the Lordship of Christ is a household that looks to the Word of God for guidance and direction.

For some couples the Bible is an ornament sitting on the coffee table in order to give just the right tasteful touch to the decor of the family den. For others the Bible serves as a convenient file drawer for important announcements, newspaper clippings, and even an occasional pressed flower—perhaps left over from a bridal bouquet. For the Christian couple the Bible is the Word of God. It is God revealing Himself in His only book. It is God speaking to the challenges of daily living. It is the Word of the Lord speaking to open ears, open hearts, and open lives. God's Word is the source of strength and power for the Christian couple who submit themselves to it.

When Jesus Christ is Lord, when He is Head of the household, the bride and groom live in the waters of their baptisms. For the Christian couple Baptism is an event and much more! It is that event in which God claimed them as His children. It is the event in which their sins were washed away and their lives were made clean before God.

Beyond the event, Baptism for the Christian couple is a life-style. They remember that Baptism is more than the memory of an event. It is the reminder that the Lord of the household forgives every day. Living in the waters of their baptisms, the Christian couple lives in a household permeated with the forgiveness of Christ. The privilege of forgiveness frees them to be submissive to one another and to their Boss, the Lord of their marriage.

As the Christian couple approaches the Lord's Supper, they submit to God in repentance—the act of turning away from the selfishness of sin. As the Lord Jesus Christ pours out His body and blood, He seals His promise to heal their hurts, strengthen their faith, and erase their mistakes.

These are the tools of a Christian marriage. These are the channels of God's grace for the household where husbands and wives submit to one another because Jesus Christ is Lord. Amen.

Kent R. Hunter

Related Scripture Readings

Mark 9:35 | 2 Cor. 11:2 | Col. 3:18-4:1 | Rev. 19:6-9
1 Cor. 13 | Phil. 2:1-11 | James 4:7-10

Suggested Hymns

"O Father, All Creating"
"The Voice That Breathed O'er Eden"
"O Perfect Love"
"O Blessed Home Where Man and Wife"
"Oh, Blest the House, Whate'er Befall"
"Take My Life that It May Be"
"Let Us Ever Walk with Jesus"
"Come, Follow Me, the Savior Spake"

WEDDING

Loved to Love

EPH. 4:32

Someone once quipped: "Broken marriages are as common as broken window panes." Unfortunately, the truth of that statement is tragically confirmed by many divorce court statistics. It remains a sad commentary on contemporary life that the high hopes and solemn promises of the wedding day are repeatedly dashed to pieces in the trials of daily living. Our age is not the first, however, to experience this reality. Writing approximately 450 years ago, Martin Luther lamented that every day marriages were "broken by the devil through adultery, unfaithfulness, discord, and all manner of ill" (*Luther's Works,* American Edition, Vol. 53, p. 113).

In the face of these gloomy facts there comes from the religious bookseller's shelf a little volume with the rather hopeful title: *Make Yours a Happy Marriage.* That book does not present an impossible dream. Marriages can be happy. God wants them to be so.

The words of our text show how it can be done:

Loved to Love

I. God's Love in Action

Successful ventures are often built on good foundations. If marriages are to be successful, then they too should rest on solid substructures. God's love in action provides precisely that kind of groundwork.

God intended a perfect world and created the same. The home of Adam and Eve has been called Paradise. In it there was no flaw, no ugliness, no strife. However, our first parents took of the forbidden fruit and passed on to all their descendants a corrupted human will. That sinful nature, which each of us has inherited, expresses itself in all sorts of base actions. In the verse before our text the apostle Paul lists some of them: bitterness, wrath, anger, slander, malice. With such things God's perfect world has been marred.

Having acted in love to create man, God acted again to redeem the human race from its sad lot. Martin Luther put it this way in one of his hymns:

God beheld my wretched state
Before the world's foundation,
And, mindful of His mercies great,
He planned my soul's salvation.
(*The Lutheran Hymnal,* No. 387, st. 4)

God gave nothing less than His own Son to free humanity from the curse of sin. That Son took upon Himself human flesh and blood. As both God and man He suffered and died, broke the bonds of death on the day of resurrection, and returned to heaven with the Father's will accomplished.

The treasury of blessings obtained by this work of Jesus Christ, the Son of God, is described with but a few words in our text: "God in Christ forgave you." That is the foundation on which Christians build their marriages. Both bride and groom live in the knowledge that they are redeemed people of God. Both are at peace with God because their sin has been forgiven in Christ Jesus. Their relationship with God gives direction to the relationships which Christians have with each other in marriage.

Since God is unchangeable, His promises of forgiveness in Christ do not change either. It is possible, however, for husband and wife to undermine that foundation in their lives. That happens when both or either marriage partner becomes careless with God's ways of maintaining His foundation in the individual life. For all too many the church is an important place to be on the wedding day, but that same sanctuary is forgotten or given only a minor role once the married life has settled down to routine. Some seem to think that the church's message of sin forgiven and peace with God in Christ is a message not too relevant to the daily tasks of life. In fact, however, no message is more relevant to the realities of life. Jesus once said: "Apart from Me you can do nothing" (John 15:5). From Christ will flow every good word and work in our daily lives. The married couple that makes churchgoing a regular practice remains in touch with the Lord's most vital communication to the world: "God in Christ forgave you." That message informs us that the almighty God has loved us in a special way. Loved by Him, we learn how to love each other.

II. Human Love in Action

Love toward each other is urged upon us by Paul in these words: "Be kind to one another, tenderhearted, forgiving one another." Such advice is good for any number of situations, but it makes an especially good motto for marriage, for the home should be a haven of peace and contentment. Kindness, compassion, and a readiness to forgive contribute to that kind of atmosphere.

Upon examination it becomes apparent that these three qualities have a major ingredient in common. They all look away from self to the needs and well-being of the other person. That kind of attitude is necessary for a successful and happy marriage and is a reflection of God's love for us. In marriage the I and the you merge into a we, and because of the we, the you in marriage takes on a significance never before seen by the I. Christian husbands and wives should work daily at reducing selfishness in order to foster the happiness of the partner.

The first of Paul's trio of Christian actions to be practiced in marriage is kindness: "Be kind to one another." The kindness here spoken of is the kindness that expresses itself in being helpful. Helpfulness is a fundamental purpose in the very institution of marriage. When the Lord God created woman He did so, Holy Scripture tells us, because Adam needed a helper with whom he might manage God's beautiful creation. Marriage rests on God's desire to provide a social unit in which mutual helpfulness might be both practiced and enjoyed. Marriage is lived within the Lord's intent, therefore, when such helpfulness becomes characteristic of the home.

Courting couples often try to conduct themselves in a spirit of helpfulness to one another by performing various kinds of little acts. The man courteously opens the car door for his girl friend. She responds with a polite thank you, and when there is an occasion to buy a gift she looks hard for something he both likes and can use.

Such little courtesies need not vanish with the wedding day, of course, but within marriage the opportunities for mutual helpfulness are far greater. Husbands and wives are to be helpful to one another in their common family goals and endeavors. It is not degrading for a husband, therefore, to pick up a dish towel, to help with getting the children ready for bed, to run an errand to the grocery store for an item forgotten by his wife on her shopping trip. A wife, on the other hand, will seek to be helpful by providing a home environment which reduces the pressures and burdens of the work world. If she is a careful shopper and a good home manager, she has become most helpful to her husband and is, as the writer of the Book of Proverbs declares, "a good wife . . . far more precious than jewels" (Prov. 31:10). And if each shares with the other useful information and insights, then the spirit of helpfulness is alive. Loved by God in Christ, such a couple is loving each other in the spirit of our Redeemer God.

To his advice to be kind and helpful Paul also adds another bit of counsel: "Be tenderhearted." That means, be compassionate, share with tender and loving concern the feelings of your marriage partner. In his Letter to the Romans Paul puts it in these terms: "Rejoice with those who rejoice, weep with those who weep" (Rom. 12:15).

Some days in life have the brightness of a summer day; others carry heartache and pain. We have our moods, moods which at times we are unable even to explain. The compassionate heart recognizes and is sensitive to these aspects of human emotion. Some situations call for a word of encouragement, others for a moment of listening, and some for no more perhaps than just a gentle touch which in effect says, "I care." How essential for husband and wife to cultivate that compassionate Christlike spirit!

Of the many things which can easily destroy the spirit of compassion, the tongue stands among the foremost. For that reason, the warning of James (3:5) deserves our ear: "The tongue is a little member and boasts of great things. How great a forest is set ablaze by a small fire!" Unkind words hurt, disfigure, and consume beautiful relationships. Such words, therefore, have no place between husband and wife. When Paul encourages us to be tenderhearted, he is suggesting that we guard our tongue so that we do not use words that set a forest ablaze.

The compassion which husband and wife show toward each other should extend as well to any children who might come to the marriage union. To give life to another human being is a marvelous privilege granted by the Lord of life to husband and wife. But the rearing of children does make special demands upon parents. In his very earthy way Martin Luther once said to one of his youngsters: "Child, what have you done that I should love you so. You have disturbed the whole household with your bawling" (Roland H. Bainton, *Here I Stand,* p. 300). Patience, control of temper, and a compassionate understanding of the complexities of growing from childhood to adulthood are Christian virtues to be cultivated by parents. Tragic cases of child abuse in contemporary society vividly demonstrate how these virtues have disintegrated in some homes. Christian parents take up the responsibilities of child rearing in the spirit of tenderheartedness. Recognizing that we have been loved by God in Christ, we are motivated to love our children with a tenderness which mirrors the kindness of our Savior.

But who can achieve Paul's ideals perfectly? No husband. No wife. Each will fail many times. Precisely for that reason Paul adds one more essential admonition: "Forgive one another as God in Christ forgave you." As the Lord pardons us daily, so we are to forgive one another.

To forgive is difficult because it is not a natural trait for sinful human beings. To forgive comes hard because we readily see the faults of others but are so often ignorant of our own. To forgive is not easy because we are too frequently misled into thinking that we have been right in our actions when in fact we were wrong. To forgive, however, is a Christian grace and one in which we should grow daily in our lives together. Then our homes will become increasingly Christlike.

Marriage counselors have much advice to give to help people live happily in marriage. The advice is often sane and sensible. Advice, however, is not all that is needed to make a happy marriage. We need motivational power to live out the advice. God's message of forgiveness in Christ is that kind of force. Daily recalling that God has forgiven us in Christ, we are empowered to be kind, tenderhearted, and forgiving to one another. That makes for a happy marriage.

Wayne E. Schmidt

Related Scripture Readings

Ps. 33:1-12 Prov. 3:1-6 John 15:1-5 1 Cor. 13

Suggested Hymns

"May We Thy Precepts, Lord, Fulfil"
"With the Lord Begin Thy Task"
"Love in Christ Is Strong and Living"